PRINCIPLED
SELLING

DAVID TOVEY

PRINCIPLED SELLING

HOW TO WIN MORE BUSINESS WITHOUT SELLING YOUR SOUL

KoganPage

LONDON PHILADELPHIA NEW DELHI

First published in Great Britain and the United States in 2012 by Kogan Page Limited

120 Pentonville Road	1518 Walnut Street, Suite 1100	4737/23 Ansari Road
London N1 9JN	Philadelphia PA 19102	Daryaganj
United Kingdom	USA	New Delhi 110002
www.koganpage.com		India

© David Tovey, 2012

ISBN   978 0 7494 6657 2
E-ISBN 978 0 7494 6658 9

British Library Cataloguing-in-Publication Data

A CIP record for this book is available from the British Library.

Library of Congress Cataloging-in-Publication Data

Tovey, David.
    Principled selling : how to win more business without selling your soul / David Tovey.
        p. cm.
    ISBN 978-0-7494-6657-2 – ISBN 978-0-7494-6658-9   1. Selling.   I. Title.
    HF5438.25.T68 2012
    658.85–dc23
                                                                              2012030708

Typeset by Graphicraft Limited, Hong Kong
Print production by Jellyfish
Printed and bound by CPI Group (UK) Ltd, Croydon, CR0 4YY

For Max, Claire and James
My most cherished and important relationships

CONTENTS

FOREWORD

The world of sales and the world of marketing have been plagued by the same problem for at least a century. The problem historically facing sales is the tendency to view selling as a method of controlling, brow-beating, or otherwise inducing the buyer to do what the seller wants. The problem facing marketing is the tendency to propagandize – to persuade customers to do the marketer's bidding. Each has had different solutions proposed over time. However, it is rare to find a single solution to this single problem. *Principled Selling* manages to achieve that task admirably.

These problems are two sides of the same coin, with marketing playing out at mass level the dysfunction that is manifested at the personal level in selling – an all-too-narrow seller-centric motivation.

Where selling has escaped the ugliest forms of coercion, the gains have been incremental, and often due to a mechanistic breaking down of the sales process into pieces, guided by larger governing insights, eg the idea that questioning should precede solutions. Such insights get turned into processes, reinforced by CRM systems. This systematization of selling ensures that the biggest mistakes are not made, but a price is paid in the mechanization of the relationship.

Similarly, the evolution of marketing away from mass messaging has been to fine-tune the segments to which the messages are broadcast, while leaving intact the seller-centric intent at persuasion.

Both these efforts still leave us with a dual failure: an impersonal and seller-centric approach to selling.

Which brings us to *Principled Selling*. The title is quite appropriate, because while selling is frequently considered a subcomponent of marketing, in my view – and I think David Tovey's as well – the reverse is more true. All buying is personal, and all marketing is really a prelude to buying; hence the proper approach to marketing ought to start with the principles of selling; and hence David Tovey replaces 'marketing' with 'motivation'.

And so *Principled Selling* applies the same single answer to what is, after all, the same single problem: to build both sales and marketing around the buyer.

Principled Selling is based on an elegantly simple idea: sellers should adapt to what the buyer is interested in buying – in the buyer's terms, from the buyer's perspective, and in the buyer's timeframe. Call that "respect for the buyer", if you will. Respect for the buyer means the seller adheres to certain principles – simple ones like don't promise what you can't deliver, act with integrity, be transparent and authentic, and above all – have good intentions.

It is a natural and simple fact – unaltered by decades of massive systems and research – that human beings buy to a great extent emotionally. They want to have their risk lowered, they want to be respected, they want to feel an emotional commitment from the seller. If the seller behaves in those manners, it is as logical as any law of human nature that the buyer will respond reciprocally.

While not brand-new, this point of view is rare enough, and even more rarely practiced.

Which is great news for the few people and organizations who *can* practice it, because it's hugely powerful.

On the marketing side, *Principled Selling* leads with content marketing, another buyer-centric concept. Rather than persuade buyers of their interest in your message, it is better to place legitimate genuine content in front of them that is responsive to desires they already have.

The idea of "customer-centricity" has been around for ages, but continues to be undermined in application by self-orientation and mechanical inauthenticity. *Principled Selling* stands out for its insistence on the human-ness of the buyer, and the need for both sales and marketing to respect it.

Charles H Green, West Orange,
New Jersey, 2012

ABOUT THE AUTHOR

David Tovey is a popular writer and speaker. His mission is to demonstrate how selling ethically, with integrity and a conscience can help build a better, more profitable business in a way that both seller and buyer will always find comfortable. The principled approach takes out any need for cold calling or sales 'techniques', removing any suggestion of manipulation from the sales process. David and his colleagues have helped hundreds of blue-chip companies and professional service firms around the world to increase top-line profitable growth by focusing on principled selling and principled leadership. David heads up the Principled Group of companies which includes Questas Consulting, the team that helps clients to implement the principled selling approach, and Valuable Content Ltd, the content marketing specialists.

ACKNOWLEDGEMENTS

I always used to wonder why books have a section for acknowledgements, now I know. Authoring a book is a massive undertaking that can't be achieved without the support of very many people, far more than I could ever mention here.

It is a journey that starts a long time before the idea even pops into your head that you might be commissioned by a leading publisher. There are many people who have influenced me over the years and I want to mention one person who inspired me as young boy to love reading and the knowledge that can be gained from books. Marjorie Tovey gave me my first 'proper' book and it still has pride of place in my bookcase. She was one of life's special people, loved by all who knew her and I have much to thank her for.

Gary Williams, David Turner and Richard Wylie, my colleagues at Principled Group, are as passionate about principled business and Principled Selling as I am and this book could never have got off the ground without their help and support. Thank you guys!

Sonja Jefferson and Sharon Tanton my colleagues at Valuable Content Ltd, with extra special thanks to Sonja Jefferson, who was there at the birth of the *Principled Selling* book and whose advice and help has so often been above and beyond the call of duty. Heather Townsend has been an inspiration and always there to encourage me with a daily tweet and a big smile when I needed it and of course expert advice on social media.

Thanks to Liz Gooster and the team at Kogan Page for their faith in me and their encouragement. Thanks to Jon Baker, Sharon Tanton, Claire Rosling, Eli and Toby of Bright New Day, Lizzie Everard and everyone who contributed case studies and quotes.

A big thank you to my editor, Robert Watson, whose patience and considered advice has taken me from being at best a writer of articles to becoming an author. Robert has a special direct way of communicating that only those who have earned the right could ever get away with. Sometimes it has been a good thing that he works from home in Sydney, but without him I could not have a book to be proud of.

If I have missed anyone; my apologies. I am eternally grateful to all those people who have helped me make this book happen.

INTRODUCTION

Why principled selling?

In this book you won't find a single sales technique to help you 'cold call', 'close' a deal or manipulate customers in any way. You will find an approach to selling that makes winning business one of the most natural and comfortable business activities to be involved in.

The dynamics of the seller–buyer relationship are shifting so dramatically that something has to change in the way we build our businesses. If you think about it for just a few moments, you will have to admit that you've noticed the change.

A crisis of trust

It started with the banking crisis – so many long-established trusted pillars of the establishment that were and are still (in some cases) household names dashing our faith in financial organizations. Millions of people all over the world were affected not just financially but in a way that caused them to question the trust they had in the institutions that they had been loyal customers of, sometimes for a lifetime. The hurt was deep and still is; we felt let down, betrayed by people who seemed to have no principles, no values other than to look after themselves, whatever the cost.

That hurt and fallout is still being played out in our newspapers day by day – and now we have the news organizations, the very organizations that campaigned with such pomposity against the people and institutions involved, in the news themselves. *'Is there any level they won't stoop to for an edge in a story?'* one relative of an alleged 'hacked' victim said on the BBC at the height of the reporting. It seems you can't trust anyone to be straight any more.

Sure, we've all learned through the hard knocks of life to have a healthy dose of cynicism, but now it seems many people almost expect to be misled or expect everyone to try to get one over on them.

Why should this affect our businesses, why do we need to be aware?

Because for those of us who have to sell a service or a product there was already plenty of suspicion that people who 'sell' things might just say or do anything to get a sale. In an online forum I took part in a recently, one sales director said:

'The job of my sales people is to make my company look good, to put a gloss on things and win business.'

It's a view held by too many people who sell; and worse, it's a view held by people who buy – even when the seller has the best of intentions. 'Sales people' just aren't trusted.

The top earners do things differently

I've worked with some of the best sales people in the world over the past 30 years, some of the top earners. These people aren't called salespeople; they are most often described as 'professionals' – skilled technical people who would hate to be thought of as sales people but nevertheless have to, and do, win business for their firms: lots of it.

The top earners I work with don't 'sell' in the stereotypical way. They have an approach to winning business that propels them to trusted advisor status. They never, ever put a gloss on things or do anything underhand. Their attitude flies in the face of everything some people think 'sales' is all about. The best salespeople take a Principled approach to selling.

A better, more profitable way to sell

I'd like to make Principled Selling something that you do too.

This book is dedicated to what is now my mission – to demonstrate how a Principled approach to selling can help build better, more profitable businesses in a way that both seller and buyer will always find comfortable.

Whether you sell full time or need to win business as part of your role, Principled Selling will help you build trusted relationships with customers and clients. It is the only approach to winning business that will help you achieve long-term sustainable business growth.

This is a highly effective, proven approach to business development that helps you align your sales techniques with the new expectations of customers and clients. It gets people to buy from you again and again, giving you a real opportunity to get ahead of the game.

The right approach for the social media age

Principled Selling is an approach that is aligned with how people buy today. The internet and social media are having a massive effect in every marketplace and they are now serious business tools used by billions of people and millions of your potential customers. The internet is the number one way to seek information and we live in a world where individuals believe their Twitter contacts more than they believe advertising.

Dispelling the myth of the 'natural' sales person

More and more people NEED to sell, to develop business, to win new customers or clients, to hold on to existing customers and to develop new lines of business. The stereotypical salesperson as a fast talker, smooth and self-interested exists but most people don't want to be like them, and most buyers don't want to listen to them!

For most business people there is rarely any training in how best to sell – in the economic downturn they have been told to 'get out there and sell'. Inevitably, under pressure they resort to what they think selling is, based too often on the very worst sales practices.

The Principled Selling approach dispels the myths around what it takes to be a successful salesperson. At its heart is a deep understanding of how to motivate a customer to want to do business with you, never resorting to pressure, manipulation or using 'closing' to win business.

Selling ethically, with integrity and a conscience

This book is about selling ethically, with integrity and a conscience. Most of the people I meet in business want to do the right thing. They want to be trusted, to earn respect, and to do a great job for their business and their customers. As I travel and work around the world I meet brilliant technicians and professionals who are passionate about their work, who often change the world for the better by what they do. I meet salespeople who are passionate about helping their customers and who enjoy finding the right solution for them.

Intellectually every business person knows that products and services have to be sold, customers have to be found. Selling is really no more than exchanging a product or service for money. Yet, somehow, when it comes to selling, to winning business, many people, including salespeople, feel they are doing something that doesn't quite feel right. Designing a great piece of software that will help a company be hugely more productive is honourable and professional but 'selling' that same piece of software is seen as something completely different. It's not quite a nice thing to do to be 'selling'; it often causes anxiety and stress. Too many people think that the normal standards of business ethics and integrity don't apply when it comes to selling, that salespeople can't afford to have a conscience.

I meet perfectly decent, normal human beings who seem to change personality when it's time to 'sell'. At a conference in Phoenix, Arizona, a couple of years ago a business development executive for an international consultancy business said to me: *'You have to sell your soul when it comes to getting people to buy.'* She went on to tell me that it's a tough competitive world out there and you sometimes have to be prepared to put a gloss on things, to make the firm look better than it really is. When I asked if that's the way she wanted it to be she replied, *'Heck no, I hate bending the truth but it's just the way it is in sales.'*

It doesn't have to be that way.

You can win business, and many people do, without it ever feeling uncomfortable for the seller or buyer. You can sell without feeling that there is something a little unsavoury about selling, without exaggerating or putting a gloss on things and definitely without selling your soul. You can be yourself without ever having to put on an act, use sales techniques or use trickery of any kind.

Principled Selling is a comfortable, creative experience for the buyer and for the seller. When you apply the principles in this book, building trusted, profitable relationships gets easier.

Who is this book for?

Principled Selling is written for business owners, accountants, engineers, lawyers, sales managers, front-line salespeople, business development executives and anyone in any business where winning long-term relationships is key to long-term success.

You will learn how to:

- sustain long-term sales growth;
- motivate potential customers and clients to meet you and buy from you;
- maintain customer loyalty;
- create opportunities for more business with key clients;
- differentiate your business by how you sell;
- become a trusted supplier and advisor;
- use social media effectively;
- build a business development culture across your business.

Professionals, technical experts, business owners and entrepreneurs for whom selling is not a full-time activity will find this book particularly useful as a practical guide to winning more of the right type of customers, who buy the right products and services at the right price.

For those who sell as a full-time activity you will learn how to bring your approach to selling right up to date with how buyers are thinking today, how to harness the power of social media to help you win more customers and how to win more business from existing customers.

How to use this book

This book is written so that you can read from cover to cover or dip in and out. At the end of each chapter you will find Action Points – exercises to help you put into practice what you have learned.

There are three sections:

Section one: The Principled Selling Approach

● Winning more business today

● The five principles of Principled Selling

Section two: Principled Selling in Action

● The Principled Selling Growth Model

● Bringing the Growth Model to life

● M2M (motivate to meet) marketing

● Winning more business with networking and social media

● M2B (motivating customers to buy)

● M2B (motivate to buy) skills and behaviours

● Proposals and presentations that WOW!

● Principled Selling key account management

Section three: Building a Principled Selling Culture

- The Principled Organisation
- Attitude and making time for Principled Selling

Throughout you will see references to customers and clients to describe organizations or individuals who buy your products or services. From time to time the phrase 'business development' is used to describe the sales process and other marketing activities that play a part in winning business.

Success at selling is not a function of personality; it is a function of applying a disciplined sales process plus application of advanced communication skills and behaviours.

The approach works; it has helped thousands of individuals and hundreds of companies across the world to meet and exceed their sales revenue targets.

Isn't it time you became a Principled Seller?

PART ONE
THE PRINCIPLED
SELLING APPROACH

Something is happening in the world of selling. Anyone involved in winning business whether as a full-time role or as part of their wider responsibilities will have noticed that traditional approaches are not working any more. The business environment and buyer behaviour have changed but for many the way they go about winning business hasn't.

The definition of insanity is to carry on doing the same thing and expect a different result.

Albert Einstein

Business people tend to smile when they hear that quote, and even say how true it is, but then they return to their desk and continue the same routine. It is almost as if these words of wisdom apply to everyone else, not them!

Part one explores how lack of trust and the internet are influencing buyers. It then considers the opportunities to differentiate for those who are prepared to respond.

CHAPTER I

WINNING MORE BUSINESS TODAY

The things which I have seen I now can see no more.

William Wordsworth

Topics covered in this chapter

- Why trust matters more than ever
- Social media and the opportunities it offers
- A different, more principled approach to selling

Why trust matters more than ever

Trust is at an all-time low

I've been involved in winning business in the recessions of every decade since the 1970s. During all that time there has never been a tougher environment for anyone who needs to win business than the present day. It's not the recession that's different; things may feel difficult but there have been worse recessions in my business lifetime.

What is very different is that today there is a global crisis of trust and increased level of cynicism never before experienced. The internet and social media means that negative or hate comments can be instantly sent to thousands of people. No one waits for a printed newspaper; no one waits for the investigation and final report. When a cruise ship hits a rock, the world is told within two hours that the captain abandoned ship and that the passengers had not had a lifeboat drill since joining the ship. Trust is earned and is always fragile. Trust built up over decades can be lost in an instant.

Consider the banking crisis – so many long-established trusted pillars of the establishment dashing our faith in financial organizations that were and are still (in some cases) household names. Millions of people all over the world were affected not just financially but in a way that caused them to question the trust they had in institutions that they had been loyal customers of, sometimes for a lifetime. The hurt was deep and still is; we felt let down, betrayed by people who seemed to have no principles and no values other than to look after themselves, whatever the cost.

Gary Hamel, ranked the world's most influential business thinker by *Fortune Magazine*, said in a recent BBC interview that the crisis had brought the whole capitalist system into question.

That hurt and fallout is still being played out in our newspapers day by day – and now we have the news organizations that campaigned with such pomposity against the people and institutions involved in the news themselves. They seem to have betrayed a trust by taking the tactics used against celebrities to ordinary people, who found themselves in extraordinary and often painful situations. '*Is there any level they won't stoop to for an edge in a story?*' one relative of an allegedly 'hacked' victim said on the BBC news recently.

The annual Edelman Barometer of Trust measures trust across 25 countries and recently reported yet again a record decline in people's trust of governments, business and even NGOs.

It seems you can't trust anyone to be straight any more. We've all learned through the hard knocks of life to have a healthy dose of cynicism, but now it seems many people almost expect to be misled or expect everyone to try to get one over on them. The default position is to be suspicious and wary.

FIGURE 1.1 Edelman Barometer of Trust

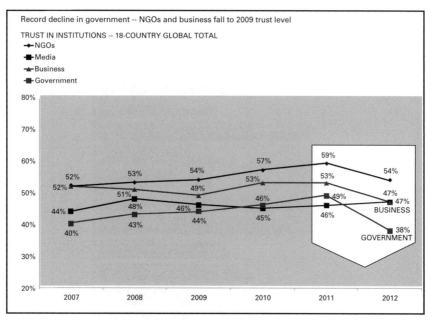

Record decline in government -- NGOs and business fall to 2009 trust level

TRUST IN INSTITUTIONS -- 18-COUNTRY GLOBAL TOTAL

In the wake of a recession that saw large, global companies such as Lehman Brothers and AIG collapse, trust in business imploded. Government stepped in with bailouts and new regulations. But then government became paralysed by the politics of extremism and endless haggling – and the public lost confidence.

Reproduced with permission of Edelman Trust

(*continued overleaf*)

Why should this affect your businesses, why do you need to be aware? Because for those of you who have to sell a service or a product there is already plenty of suspicion that people who *sell* things might just say or do anything to get a sale. Sadly the evidence is that there are still plenty of sellers out there who are prepared to do just that.

I've asked thousands of people in seminars and conferences all over the world to close their eyes, think of a typical salesperson and then describe them to me.

Take a few moments and have a go yourself. Close your eyes and get a picture in your mind of the typical salesperson. How do they look? What are they wearing? What behaviours do they exhibit? Chances are the image you

FIGURE 1.1 *continued*

Several mature markets see double-digit drops in business trust

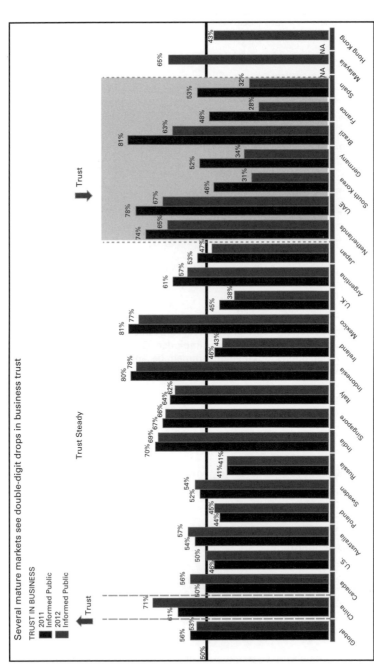

China was the only country to see a rise in trust during the last year. Banks and financial institutions remain the least trusted businesses.

Edelman Barometer of Trust

have will reflect a stereotype of the worst type of salesperson you have ever experienced.

The responses I hear are rarely complimentary and include:

- good at talking;
- doesn't listen;
- too quick at assuming familiarity;
- insincere;
- always pitching;
- uses sales techniques to manipulate;
- have their own interests at heart;
- extrovert;
- cheap shiny suit;
- always 'closing';
- pre-prepared answer for everything;
- gets annoyed if you say *no*;
- prepared to use pressure.

This isn't what professional salespeople actually do but the fact that so many people across so many countries use the same words (did you?) is a serious problem for anyone who needs to win business.

For many of you reading this book, winning business is your full-time activity. Business owners, professionals, technical experts, administrators and even many marketing professionals love what they do but many hate the idea of having to sell. I have worked with thousands of individuals who believe the myths about selling – that it is about having the right personality, about being extroverted and being able to persuade or manipulate. Some professional services firms are so uncomfortable about the 'S' word that they will not allow the word 'selling' to be used, preferring the euphemism 'business development'.

Many business people, particularly those with a technical discipline, have often described themselves to me as being 'unnatural salespeople'. If unnatural salespeople believe the myths of selling, they avoid getting involved in selling.

FIGURE 1.2   What salespeople really mean

Reproduced with permission of Guardian Newspapers

Not surprisingly, avoiding selling does not help you to grow a business. Waiting for the phone to ring has put too many companies out of business.

Critically if you believe the myths, you will put into practice what you think selling is about and will end up selling badly. Selling badly doesn't help your business to grow either.

Not everyone selling is like that of course but even when the seller has the best of intentions things have become so bad that anyone who looks like, sounds like or smells like a typical salesperson just isn't trusted. Just not listening enough can lead a buyer to suspect they are in the presence of someone who has their own self-interest at heart and not the interests of the customer.

Social media and the opportunities it offers

The internet revolution

The internet has changed everything. Fifteen years ago I toured Europe, Australia and New Zealand speaking on how to use the internet to market products and services. Websites were at best basic online brochures back then. Some had rudimentary systems to order online; the world wide web was in its infancy. There were no smart phones and the inventors of social media were still at school! There are now over two billion internet users worldwide.

People like to connect using the internet: LinkedIn is growing by over a million members each month; there are over 30 billion Tweets each year; and 180 million Facebook members log on every 24 hours.

You can add several billions of interactions more for people accessing online forums, discussion groups, videos and images on platforms such as YouTube and Flickr.

In all areas of human endeavour millions of people now turn to social media to learn who they can trust and this applies whatever you are supplying these days. Many commodity purchases that would have been transacted in a store are now made online, taking away the need for traditional sales staff. For more complex products and services the web and social media are increasingly important in building a positive reputation, building credibility, demonstrating competence and building trust.

In this new business world, even if a buyer isn't particularly social media savvy, the minimum they will do is check out a potential supplier's website. If they have an appointment with a potential supplier they will check for online profiles on websites LinkedIn, Twitter and Facebook. They are checking if the individual and their company are 'players' and if the story they tell in the online world is the same that they hear face to face. They are also seeking valuable content that will help them with their business issues even before they meet you. Cold-calling, mass marketing and telemarketing aren't working like they once did. According to a recent survey by Hot to Trot marketing, in 2006 it took only six calls from a telemarketing firm to make one contact. In 2011 it was up to 41 calls to make a contact.

The Edelman Barometer of Trust surveyed 25,000 people and asked where they go to get information they trust; the response:

- people similar to myself;
- my social networks (online and offline);
- micro-blogging sites;
- websites which share valuable content.

These sources of information saw an increase in trust of between 75 per cent and 88 per cent in 2012 (source: Edelman Barometer of Trust).

Technology and the behaviour of buyers have moved on massively. Rather than hoping social media and the internet will go away, Principled Sellers harness its power, deliver valuable content and use it to provide an even better opportunity to communicate in the way customers appreciate.

The opportunity

The implosion of trust plus the explosion of the internet and social media presents a massive opportunity. These are truly exciting times for those organizations that align their sales and marketing approach with the expectations of customers and clients.

Despite lack of trust being an almost daily news item, most companies are doing little or nothing to address the real issues. I personally experience and get to hear about poor sales approaches each and every week. Knowing I would be writing about this today I tweeted a request to my followers to ask if anyone had a recent example of what they considered to be a poor sales approach. Within minutes I received more than a dozen examples from the UK and the USA.

Sadly there are far too many out there who still give selling a bad name.

Neil Fletcher, Product Sales Manager, leading electronics firm

To protect the guilty I won't mention the name of the financial services group who one respondent said had *'really annoyed me with their pressure tactics to get my credit card details long before I was ready to buy'* or the software salesperson who gave a one-hour online demonstration to my colleague and fellow author Heather Townsend, without asking a single question. Heather was so annoyed she left the room to scream, twice!

I recently spent time with a supplier I thought my company might do business with. I sat through an excellent one-hour presentation about their company and had a very thorough tour of their facility. After three hours I departed with the supplier knowing nothing about my business. In a meeting with a large technology company the sales director told me he would never allow a technical support person to go on a sales visit with a salesperson. When I asked why, the response astonished me: *'If a customer asks a techie any questions, they always tell the truth!'*

There is still so much bad sales practice out there that it can be a major differentiator to sell in a way that doesn't make potential buyers cringe; that doesn't increase cynicism but instead builds trust.

I am both disappointed and optimistic at the same time. I'm disappointed that so many organizations still don't seem to be making the necessary changes. I'm optimistic because I know that differentiation between competitors will not be *if* they build trust and harness the internet, but *how well* they do it. There is all to play for and Principled Selling will help you win.

Buyer behaviours and attitude

We know that the world for anyone who needs to win business is changing due to low trust and the internet revolution. This is affecting buyer behaviour in subtle as well as more obvious ways.

CASE STUDY

At a procurement conference, I presented a paper on Principled Selling. The following speaker was a government procurement specialist and she challenged the audience, 'You really need to listen, because we know all about the sales techniques you use to try to sell to us.' She went on to describe the various sales techniques she and her colleagues had experienced: 'These days it's all about wanting to understand us, so salespeople use different types of questions to find the buying signals.' She then said something that I have no doubt were the most profound words I've heard from a buyer: 'I have news for you – we choose who we allow to understand us.'

She explained that she and her department of 50 professional procurement executives knew that the better salespeople were taught to show interest and get to understand the customer but that it is always obvious to them when this isn't genuine interest, just a technique used to get to a sale. She laughed about the salespeople resorting to techniques to 'find the pain' or 'what keeps you up at night' – which she said was usually interpreted as, 'How can I get an order out of you as quickly as possible?'

Salespeople all over the world are going into meetings with potential buyers and because of the way they use sales techniques they leave not fully understanding the customer's requirements because the customer chose not to share the full picture with them. Many of course will blame the customer or blame price for the buyer going to a competitor, but, as we will see later, price is rarely the real reason a sale is lost.

Not so long ago the only reference material that buyers had to check out the veracity of a potential supplier's sales and marketing message was the brochures and advertising written by the supplier. If a customer wasn't happy they would have to write in or in rare cases take part in a customer survey. Now pretty much any information about anything is available online. Reputations can be checked out using online forums, Twitter or Facebook. Before you visit a potential customer, your own profile can be checked out on LinkedIn and your website checked out. Prices can be researched, trading infringements can be viewed and competitors can be explored.

If you let a customer down today the world can know about it in seconds on Twitter or Facebook. A YouTube video made by an irate passenger about poor customer service had millions of views and as a result had a direct and negative effect on a major airline's share price. I asked an audience of students in Istanbul what they would do if a supplier let them down – in unison dozens shouted *Twitter and Facebook them.*

We know from the Edelman Barometer of Trust that people trust information and recommendations from people similar to themselves and their online social networks. Buyers seek out people who they trust (people similar to themselves) and ask for an opinion about companies, brands and even about individuals. There is nowhere for suppliers of products or services to hide and buyers know it.

It is no longer acceptable to think *caveat emptor* (let the buyer beware). Contracts and small print might absolve you of the legal responsibility to deliver on a marketing or sales message but your company and personal brand will pay the price. *Caveat emptor* shifts the risk to the buyer in a time when it is their priority to reduce risk. Today, you should be thinking *cave vendit* (seller beware), particularly in the light of prospects choosing who they allow to understand them!

People want to do business with organizations and individuals they trust, partly because it is a more pleasant way to do business but mainly because it is about reducing risk. Taking to dinner someone important who you want to impress usually means taking care to choose a restaurant that you know you can trust. You reduce the risk of a bad dining experience by choosing a venue that you feel won't let you down on an important occasion. It's the same with most business relationships. You reduce the risk to you or your business by working with a supplier you trust.

Each customer, client or prospect has their own objectives, their own critical success factors and their own problems. A decision maker is not going to have made their daily commute this morning thinking that they ought to do some business with you today because you are such nice people. They are unlikely to be thinking about your profits, cash flow, staff, clients or supplier problems. They will be thinking about their own profits, cash flow, staff, customers and supplier problems. Everybody is busy today and decision makers are busy too; too busy to deal with anything or anyone who interrupts their day. Have you noticed how few accept invites to events these days however good the wine and canapés?

Here's the deal. If you have something that will positively contribute to helping them achieve their goals, to help them address their critical success factors, then they might, just might, have time for you. Just because you believe you have the latest and best products and know you provide great customer service doesn't mean you will get any of their time or attention. Decision makers at all levels in organizations are bombarded with selling messages every day.

It has always been true that all buying decisions include emotions and logic. Buyers engage emotions at the beginning and end of the business development process and in the middle it is about ticking all the logic boxes. Salespeople have known this for many years and used sales techniques to manipulate unwary buyers to get them through each stage of the sale. Now there are very few, if any, unwary buyers. They are more cynical than ever, have access to more information than ever and insist on a genuine trusted relationship more than ever.

A different, more principled approach to selling

Time to be different

Principled Selling is about selling ethically, with integrity and a conscience. It is aligned with how people buy today and it is the only approach to winning business that will help you achieve long-term sustainable business growth.

Most of the people I meet in business want to do the right thing. They want to be trusted, to earn respect, and to do a great job for their business and their customers. As I travel and work around the world I meet brilliant technicians and professionals who are passionate about their work, who often change the world for the better by what they do. I meet salespeople who are passionate about helping their customers and who enjoy finding the right solution for them.

Intellectually every business person knows that products and services have to be sold, customers have to be found. Selling is really no more than exchanging a product or service for money.

Yet, somehow, when it comes to selling, to winning business, many people, including salespeople, feel they are doing something that doesn't quite feel right. Designing a great piece of software that will help a company be hugely more productive is honourable and professional but 'selling' that same piece of software is seen as something completely different. It's not quite a nice thing to do to be 'selling'; it often causes anxiety and stress. Too many people think that the normal standards of business ethics and integrity don't apply when it comes to selling, that salespeople can't afford to have a conscience.

I meet perfectly decent, normal human beings who seem to change personality when it's time to 'sell'. At a conference in Phoenix, Arizona, a couple of years ago a business development executive for an international consultancy business said to me 'You have to sell your soul when it comes to getting people to buy.' She went on to tell me that it's a tough competitive world out there and you sometimes have to be prepared to put a gloss on things, to make the firm look better than it really is. When I asked if that's the way she wanted it to be she replied: 'Heck no, I hate bending the truth but it's just the way it is in sales.'

It doesn't have to be that way.

You can win business and many people do, without it ever feeling uncomfortable for the seller or buyer. You can sell without feeling that there is something a little unsavoury about selling, without exaggerating or putting a gloss on things and definitely without selling your soul. You can be yourself without ever having to put on an act, use sales techniques or trickery of any kind.

When you apply Principled Selling, building trusted relationships gets easier.

Principled Selling is about selling ethically

You only really notice someone is 'selling' to you when they are selling unethically, usually trying to persuade you to buy something that you don't really want. When someone sells you something you want, you hardly notice what is going on because you are motivated to buy. As unethical selling is usually to the buyer's detriment, many people end up considering all selling to be slightly distasteful because they tend to remember the techniques and tricks used by poor sellers.

Selling ethically simply means identifying a situation where your product or service matches a customer's requirements. This involves asking relevant questions, listening to the customer, exploring potential solutions and providing information in an understandable way so that the customer can make an informed decision. Selling ethically focuses on the customer and their requirements, not on the need of the seller to generate a sale.

Unethical selling is sometimes obvious and easily recognizable. Television abounds with rouge trader and 'rip-off' programmes. Sometimes it is more subtle. False deadlines to make a decision, up-selling an insurance policy just for the higher commission, using fear of crime to persuade a vulnerable person to buy a security system they don't need, the pretence of seeking permission of a superior to give a discount if the deal is closed today.

Selling ethically requires advanced communication skills and the ability to ask the right insightful questions, to *really* listen (the toughest selling skill of all) and to provide information that is relevant. The skilled seller has to have the ability to ask insightful questions, to challenge and to present information logically, clearly and in a way adapted to suit the customer. It also means being able to challenge a customer when the seller is professionally concerned that they might not make the best decision. Challenging the customer doesn't mean arguing with them, by the way. Principled Sellers earn the right to challenge by building trust. When you have earned the right to challenge you become a trusted advisor and supplier.

Principled Selling is about selling with integrity

To have integrity is to act according to the values, beliefs and principles a person claims to hold. Principled Selling involves selling ethically and therefore integrity is about the honesty, truthfulness and accuracy of the sellers' actions. The opposite of integrity is inconsistency and hypocrisy – claiming to have one set of values, beliefs and principles yet failing to consistently act in accordance with them.

When a seller makes claims on their website that they provide a no quibble money back guarantee and a customer wants their money back, behaving with integrity means they get it every time. When a professional says they will never do any work that will incur fees without clearing them with the clients first, behaving with integrity means that's what they do every time. When a salesperson assures a customer that they are passionate about great customer service, integrity means they are consistently passionate about customer service.

Having integrity is easy on good days, when things are going well and there are no difficult choices to make. The real test is on those difficult days when behaving in a way that is consistent with your proclaimed values has a perceived cost. Every one of the corporations and financial institutions that let us down during the banking crisis had fine sounding values and corporate social responsibility policies prominently displayed on their websites and in their marketing materials. The problem was not the proclaimed values and principles; it was that some of them had no integrity.

Principled Selling is about selling with a conscience

Selling with a conscience is about doing the right thing for your customer **and** the right thing for your own organization. Good conscience is when you know your actions were inherently the right ones to take. Bad conscience is that feeling of guilt or remorse at not having done the right thing.

If you have a situation where it is clear to you that you cannot deliver on a client's expectations, doing the right thing is about pointing them in a direction where they could be better served, even if doing so means turning down the order and sending them to a competitor. The payback for doing the right thing is the trust you build with your customer.

CASE STUDY

'During a first meeting with a prospect, who had been referred to me by a good client of mine, I was asked if we could deliver a management development programme for trainees. It was a significant programme involving hundreds of staff. Although not a core expertise for us I found myself thinking, just for a moment, that I could maybe subcontract the programme to another provider with the right skills and deliver it under our name. That wasn't the right thing to do. The right thing to do was to let the prospect know it wasn't something we did and suggest a couple of providers they might talk with. I left the meeting feeling good but with no business!

'A couple of weeks later the client who had referred me called to say how impressed the prospect had been with my approach. It turned out that the prospect was a major customer of theirs. I was called in for a joint meeting with my client and the prospect to discuss a project that was perfect for us – and I walked out of that meeting with a six-month project involving them both. They didn't bother to talk to any other providers. In my experience doing the right thing always pays off.'

Richard Wylie, CEO, Principled Group Ltd

A few days ago I was working with a team of really bright account managers from a leading information security business. We were discussing selling and I had been sharing the information I've shared with you in this chapter. After about 30 minutes or so one account manager said: 'Yes, I agree with all that but at the end of the day it's the salesperson's job to manipulate the situation to their advantage and get prospects to do what they want them to do.' Fortunately I'm very patient!

The old perception of what selling is about is so embedded that too many full-time salespeople believe that it's how you should go about winning business and so do too many others for whom selling is something they get involved in reluctantly. The stereotypical salesperson, sales techniques and trickery do exist. Buyers are right to be more cynical and less trusting. Just this morning

I read a Tweet from a sales training organization providing a link to an article on how to sell something you don't believe in!

If you visit online selling forums you will read post after post from salespeople and their managers complaining that *something is going on*. You will see clients and customers being castigated for being more difficult to get appointments with, more price conscious, more demanding and more difficult. You will see complaints about social media being a *fad* and interfering with the good old-fashioned job of selling. For those who have used a traditional approach to selling it must indeed be a difficult time. They are not being helped by even the sales training still available by global providers and the books promising magic bullet solutions to making the next sale.

Go to YouTube and you can watch a training video from a well-known sales training provider that will tell you that all customers lie and that it is the job of a salesperson to get to the source of their business pain as quickly as possible and sell a solution. Another sales training organization actively promotes manipulating situations to your advantage. You can buy selling books promising to show you the latest psychological technique guaranteed to get you the sale. There are countless books on how to stay motivated as a salesperson and how you can stay positive in the face of all those rejections.

A client gave me a different version of the Einstein quote I have already referred to: 'If you always do what you always did you probably won't even get what you did get.' I agree with the sentiment. Before any of the processes, skills and behaviours of Principled Selling will work for you, you need to have the right mindset about selling. If you start with a mindset like that of the account manager mentioned above or if you think that standards of doing business somehow change when selling, then you will be unlikely to put into practice any of what is contained in this book.

Something is *going on*

I'm pressing this point because Principled Selling will work for you only if you start with the mindset that you want to do business in an ethical way, with integrity and a conscience. It will work for you if you are trustworthy and want to do the best for your customers and clients. Principled Selling will work for you if you believe in your product or service and deliver on your promises.

Today, however, it is no longer enough to *be* honest and trustworthy. Most people in business are honest and trustworthy; they want to do a great job for their customers and clients. Most have an excellent product or service. But broadcasting a message, shouting from the rooftops about how honest you are or how brilliant your products and services are ironically works against you, not for you. Today selling needs to be a *conscious competence*, so that you know how your words and behaviours contribute to building trusting relationships. This requires not only that you are genuine but that you demonstrate that throughout the business development process from marketing to winning new customers to developing existing relationships. You need to know why selling meetings have gone well and you need to know why things have gone wrong with your approach, presentation or proposal.

You have the opportunity to differentiate your business by how you sell. You have the opportunity to stand out from your competitors because you know how to build trust. You have the opportunity to sustain long-term profitable growth by taking a new approach to selling – Principled Selling.

In Chapter 2 I will share with you more about the Principled Selling mindset and the five Principles that will help you to win more business.

Summary

The business landscape has changed for anyone who needs to win business. Trust matters more than ever before because cynicism towards people who sell has never been so high. Even salespeople don't like being in sales any more! Unfortunately a few stereotypical salespeople perpetuate the myth that selling is somehow a distasteful thing to do, not quite a nice thing to do, and that to be involved in selling is somehow demeaning. Yet selling is no more than exchanging goods and services for money and there is a fantastic opportunity for those who adopt Principled Selling and who understand how to use social media to build trust. Most people in business do want to do what is best for their customers as well as their own organization but it isn't enough to have good intentions; today you have to demonstrate that you can be trusted – *before* anyone will entertain buying from you. What is needed for the future is a different, more principled approach to selling.

Action points

- Review your own and your team's thinking about selling. Are you or any of your team failing to win business because you believe the myths about what selling really is?

- Check your website and your marketing materials to see what they say about your company's values and principles.

- Take a reality check – ask if you and your team consistently demonstrate your organization's values and principles.

- Check your top-five competitors' websites for their values and ask your colleagues how well those companies demonstrate them.

- Review your own and your team's attitude to and involvement with social media. Have you fully harnessed the power of the internet to help you win business?

- Discuss, with colleagues, anything that might need to change in your organization to enable you to sell ethically, with integrity and a conscience.

- Check out the resources section at **www.principledgroup.com/resources**.

CHAPTER 2

THE FIVE PRINCIPLES OF PRINCIPLED SELLING

> *In a networked world, trust is the most important currency.*

Eric Schmidt

In the previous chapter we looked at why a new approach to selling is needed by anyone who wants to grow a business based on winning long-term profitable relationships. In this chapter I will introduce you to the five Principles that make Principled Selling work, why they work and how to apply them. The five Principles, when practised together, will help you to sell ethically, with integrity and a conscience.

Topics covered in this chapter

- What selling is *really* about
- Building relationships based on trust
- Being the real you

> **The five principles**
>
> - Selling is about motivation not manipulation.
> - Profitable relationships require investment.
> - There must be congruency throughout the business development process.
> - Long-term relationships depend on being authentic.
> - Being human gets results.

What selling is *really* about

Principle 1 – selling is about motivation not manipulation

A core Principled Selling behaviour is to be a master of *motivation* not manipulation. Let's take a look at why manipulation is not a useful behaviour.

In Chapter 1, I mentioned the account manager who told me that selling was about manipulating situations to your advantage. Too many salespeople have been trained to manipulate and too many individuals who need to win business believe you have to be manipulative to sell.

CASE STUDY

'On a plane recently I was trapped next to a machine tool salesman who told me he loved the personal challenge of manipulating customers around to his way of thinking. It made me cringe.'

Chris Stephens, Senior VP Marketing, UK telecoms company

Some people do seem to take pride in getting their own way whether their way is good for the other party in a relationship or not; they simply like to be in control. Manipulation is about control, in the worst sense of the word. The definition of manipulation is 'to control or influence unscrupulously'.

I spoke with a successful recruitment consultant at a networking event who told me she was planning to leave her firm because every day her director told the team to keep control of the client relationship. Even when it was obvious that the client was not sure about a candidate or a candidate was unsure about taking up a new role, her director's mantra about staying in control was interpreted by the team as doing or saying pretty much anything that would result in getting the commission.

Relationships don't work well if either party is constantly working to their own agenda, working in their own interests instead of the interests of the relationship. Most readers will have heard of going for the win-win in any negotiation. It is simply impossible to achieve win-win if one party uses manipulation to achieve their objectives.

I feel sure you, like most people, can tell if someone tries to manipulate you. In business, customers will usually be too polite to point out that they feel the seller is being unscrupulous; they just don't buy. For the few that do buy, buyer's remorse is more frequent when they discover that they have been manipulated.

The definition of selling is *the exchange of goods and services for money*. Yet when I ask groups I work with at seminars and conferences how they define selling; they often use words like *persuade* or *convince*. They say it's about getting someone to do what you want them to do. Think of how it feels when someone is trying to *persuade* or *convince* you of something. Persuasion suggests argument or coercion. It may be OK for the debating chambers of fine universities or between government politicians where rhetoric is valued, but when you want to win long-term relationships with clients it isn't helpful.

Think of the words, tone and body language of someone who is trying to persuade or convince someone. There is a tendency to repeat and reinforce the words and even to get animated. If you don't see things their way quickly enough, their voice gets louder and their hand gestures and body language can become intimidating. You feel pressured. Think of how many times you hear the term *pressure selling*. In selling situations when an individual feels pressurized their initial response is usually to push back a little. Salespeople call this push back *raising objections* and as they have heard them all before they have ready answers. Then there are the closing techniques to get you at a moment of weakness when you run out of objections. I have a book on my desk right now that advises salespeople to 'always be closing'!

Anyone who uses pressure, persuasion or convincing to attempt to win business will at best end up with a single transaction. It is not a good foundation for developing long-term profitable relationships with customers.

When you think that selling is about controlling or manipulating, all the energy in a relationship will come from you. It will be obvious that the relationship is about what you want, not what the customer wants. Selling like this feels adversarial and is usually not enjoyable or comfortable for either party.

As I researched books on selling I found that many still focus on salespeople's attitudes, how to find pain points and how to use psychological techniques to get others to do what you want. There are so many books, courses and motivational speakers encouraging bad practice that it is no wonder that anyone who needs to win business might feel they have to suspend ethics, integrity and their conscience. If a potential customer identifies bad sales practice at the start of a relationship, they will assume that this behaviour represents what it will be like to do business with a supplier once they become a client.

Be a master of motivation

When you are a master of motivation the energy will come from the customer and the whole process of selling becomes a more enjoyable and comfortable experience for seller and buyer.

Imagine only ever meeting buyers who are motivated to take a call from you, who look forward to meeting you and who look forward to your proposal or presentation. Imagine a buyer so motivated to buy from you that they give you advice on how best to sell to their company and how to construct your proposal or presentation for maximum effect. That is what happens for Principled Sellers.

When you are selling to motivated customers there is no need for manipulation, sales trickery, cold-calling or closing techniques.

CASE STUDY

'I only want to spend my time with potential clients who are interested in meeting me and with whom I can build a great working relationship. I personally don't want to go through the pain of making phone calls to people who just see me as an interruption to their day and want to get me off the phone as quickly as possible. When I call someone, I love the fact that they are expecting my call. It means I never put off making a call to a completely new prospect. When I meet a prospective client it is because they have willingly given up time to explore opportunities for doing business together. It is the most natural thing in the world to have a conversation about business with someone who is motivated to meet with you. If there are genuine opportunities to do business it is the clients' motivation that will drive the discussions forward. Instead of chasing them they call me, they want to do business, they set the pace. I used to say I could never sell, but I've found out it is easier and more enjoyable than I thought.'

Jim Stafford, Forensic Accountant, Edinburgh

A motivated client will be enthusiastic about taking action; the energy to move forward will come from them. Your marketing activities motivate a potential customer to want to meet with you and maintaining momentum throughout the business development process will motivate them to buy from you.

For most suppliers of a product or service there will be a number of stages to go through before getting a *yes*.

FIGURE 2.1   From prospect to customer

The time taken to move from a marketing approach to getting the *yes* will be different depending on your product or service. For some it may be weeks, for others it may be months; if you happen to sell defence systems it may be several years. It is not unusual for professionals in law or accountancy to tell me that it has taken several years to attract their very best clients.

If we think of the stages as necessary steps towards winning business, then it is vital that the buyer and seller are on the same step before attempting to move forward. Too often there is a mismatch between where the seller thinks the sale is and where the buyer really is. The seller is asked at the end of a first meeting to put something in writing and may think that the prospect is ready to buy. In reality the prospect may be being polite and is bringing the meeting to a close in what they think is a courteous way. The seller pulls out all the stops to get a proposal out, and when it lands on the prospect's desk it isn't opened for days or even weeks. The risk is that the seller starts to follow up too soon, starts to apply what is perceived as pressure and any motivation that might have been present disappears.

If you ever feel you are pushing or pulling them up those steps, then you can be sure that you have failed to motivate them. Motivated buyers go hand in hand with you through the business development process. You are always on the same step as each other and always feel comfortable about moving forward together to the next stage.

Principled Selling Tip: Become a master of motivation.

Building relationships based on trust

Principle 2 – Profitable relationships require investment

Many years ago when I was given the opportunity to start a new business for a UK plc my main board director said, 'David, always remember that turnover is vanity, profit is sanity.' Simple but wise words to which I would only add that it is cashflow that can more easily make or break a business.

Achieving your sales growth ambitions starts with identifying the types of customers that will generate the income for the future state you would like your business to be in. Too often businesses are reacting to opportunities and will take whatever business comes their way, often without knowing if the relationship will be profitable. I have been amazed by how even very large corporations take on projects not knowing whether they will make a profit.

CASE STUDY

'We were in negotiation with a local authority to deliver an infrastructure project. It was of significant value and just over a year's worth of work for one of our teams. It became fairly obvious at an early stage that what was being asked for wasn't actually a specialism for us. We had never delivered this type of project before but we were told by head office we needed to win the business. We trimmed the price to the bone, made promises and won the contract. It ended up being a nightmare. There was no way we could deliver the project for the price we went in at, so we cut corners and the client was furious. We lost an awful lot of money on that project. We didn't do work with that client again. I was made redundant after head office decided to close the regional office.'

Simon Carter, Consulting Engineer, global engineering consultancy

There may be circumstances from time to time where a conscious and deliberate decision is made to trim profit on a particular transaction in return for longer-term profitable growth. When such a decision is made you must be totally confident that you can deliver in full on the promises you make. To enter into a contract fully aware that you are unable to make sufficient money to deliver as promised is clearly not ethical; it will destroy trust and make it more difficult to achieve sales growth.

There's nothing new when it comes to relationships!

Any relationship that is important to you, business or personal, needs your investment. Most of that investment will be time, effort and thought. Investing in business relationships is about what you put in before expecting anything in return. In a world where trust is at a premium this is more important to Principled Sellers than ever.

The McGraw-Hill advert first appeared in *Business Week* in 1958 – over 50 years ago! The moral of the ad's story was relevant then and it is even more relevant today: *build relationships before you try to sell*. Many business cultures across the world depend on building sound relationships before discussing business.

FIGURE 2.2   Build relationships before you sell

"I don't know who you are.
I don't know your company.
I don't know your company's product.
I don't know what your company stands for.
I don't know your company's customers.
I don't know your company's record.
I don't know your company's reputation.
Now–what was it you wanted to sell me?"

MORAL: Sales start **before** your salesman calls–with business publication advertising.

McGRAW-HILL MAGAZINES
BUSINESS • PROFESSIONAL • TECHNICAL

All reasonable attempts were made to secure permission for inclusion of this quote/image. If you are the holder of the rights to this quote/image please contact us immediately. We will continue to endeavour to secure permission for use of this quote/image in any further reprints of this book.

It may take several meetings in China or Turkey for instance before you will be trusted enough to discuss business potential. This is why so many Western European and US companies fail to secure business in these cultures. Three-week selling trips, packing in dozens of appointments to pitch for business usually fail miserably because there is no attempt to build a relationship before attempting to win business.

In the boom years and before the crisis of trust, broadcasting a sales message was enough to generate an enquiry. All the investment then went into corporate marketing, advertising, PR and maybe hospitality. Those were the days of mass marketing and cold-calling. Sales appointments were about telling your product, service or company story, finding the customer's pain points, looking for buying signals and closing the deal. There was no cooperation between sales teams and marketing, between fee earners and business development departments. I'm not sure the approach was ever really successful, but it certainly isn't successful now.

There is a time in the business development process when it is your turn to enthusiastically and with passion tell your story – but too often solutions or proposals are presented prematurely. Pitching starts before the prospect is motivated to buy, or before the seller has earned the right to move the sale forward.

If you want to build long-term relationships with customers who buy and re-buy, you need to earn the right to meet with decision makers, earn the right to get to know them, earn the right to move the sales process forward to the next logical stage and earn the right to present your solution. The good news is that you have so many more tools available to help you to build relationships.

Principled Selling Tip: Earn the right to move the sale forward.

In Chapter 3 you will learn how to use valuable content to build trust, to build relationships and to motivate your prospects to meet you. You will be introduced to the Principled Selling M2M (motivate to meet) and M2B (motivate to buy) processes that will increase your sales effectiveness and your profit.

Being the real you

Principle 3 – There must be congruency throughout the business development process

The term 'business development' has increasingly become a way to describe what used to be called selling. Instead of sales executives, there are now business development executives. In sectors where 'selling' is perceived as too harsh a word to describe attracting new clients, business development is used to describe the sales process.

In Principled Selling, business development is the term used to describe everything that an organization needs to do in order to grow their sales revenue. It includes marketing, PR, face-to-face selling, proposals, tenders, presentations, pitches, customer service, developing relationships and new opportunities with current clients. In some organizations one person fulfills all those roles. In others there may be several departments and many people who make a contribution.

Congruence is derived from the Latin word *congruo* meaning *to agree*. Principled Selling requires agreement between all parts of your business development process.

- Your selling behaviours have to be congruent with the expectations set by your marketing messages.
- Your selling messages must be congruent with your marketing messages.
- The delivery of your product or service must be congruent with the promises made both marketing and sales activity.
- You must act in congruence with your own values.
- You must act in congruence with the stated values of your organization.

Whenever there is a mismatch between an individual or an organization saying one thing but deliberately doing another, a long-term relationship built on trust is impossible.

CASE STUDY

'I rarely look at brochures or newsletters any more. Most of them are full of the story the supplier wants me to hear. Even websites are just full of marketing information. They are designed to make the suppliers' product or service look better than they really are. Maybe at one time I would accept that marketing would jazz things up a bit, use a bit of marketing licence. I used to find myself thinking they would say that. Now I ask for recommendations for suppliers I can trust. I check out what customers say about suppliers on social networking sites.'

Stephen Hales, Director, creative design company

On a train out of London I overheard a conversation between two people from a leading software company. I knew they were from the same company because they were still displaying their security passes on a chain around their neck.

It was clear that one was from sales and the other from technical support – the giveaway was when their conversation went like this:

'The thing is Rob, the customer expects me to tell her that we will deliver on time and it will be fully functional this time, but then I'm from Sales so she'd expect me to be bullish. On the other hand you are not Sales and when you say something it's more likely to believed.'

To which Rob replied:

'I'd like to help you out but I don't want to sound like a salesperson or I'd lose any credibility I have got.'

It amazes me that this sort of thinking is still around in a major technology business. I checked out the website of the company and it mentioned customers being at the heart of everything they do, providing the right solution, on time and on specification. Nowhere could I find that they don't want you to meet their technical support people until after the sales department has closed the deal. There are probably some HR policies that the company could point to that discourages unethical practices, but it's what the customer experiences that they will measure you by, not the words. We tend to measure ourselves by our intentions; customers measure us by our actions.

If you ever find yourself feeling uncomfortable about your product or service being able to match the expectations of your customers, it is likely that you are acting out-of-congruence with your personal values or beliefs. When your behaviours lack congruency with your personal beliefs customers can tell. They will see it in your face and body language; they will hear it in your voice. While I did recently see a course being offered for salespeople who don't believe in their products, I can only assume the company was offering acting lessons!

Principle 4 – Long-term relationships depend on being authentic

Being authentic is more than being honest. Honesty in business can sometimes suggest a sense of having never knowingly told an untruth. Authenticity implies a lack of attempt to manipulate another person's perception. It means letting others see us as we are, and that we strive to ensure everyone's perception of us is the same.

CASE STUDY

'Behaving with integrity is a way of life. It's got nothing to do with the context, selling or any other. When you're asked, 'Were you honest?' it's a bit like being asked, 'Did you sneeze?' It's either 'Yes' or it's 'No'. 'Kind of' just doesn't cut it – it's not authentic.

Barry Jackson, Director, Aspire Academy

Being authentic when you are a Principled Seller means actually possessing the attributes or characteristics you claim or demonstrate. It means you are sincere, free from hypocrisy or dishonesty and that you are true to your own personality and character. Being authentic makes being congruent throughout the business development process easy.

When you listen to a prospect your interest needs to be genuine, not put on in order to seduce your potential customer into believing you really care. It becomes easy and more enjoyable for you and the prospect when you *do* care and when you *are* interested. It will also be more profitable for you.

You know when someone is being insincere and so do your clients. You will probably have met people in your career who can be quite good at convincing others of their sincerity and apparent genuine interest. They can be good at using listening or trust as techniques to achieve their own objectives. In every case those same people find it hugely difficult to build long-term trusted relationships because their lack of authenticity is soon found out. They may have relationships but their lack of sincerity is found out because they soon lose interest once they have what they want. I was speaking with a group of lawyers about this when one of them asked if he had to be genuinely interested in all of his clients. My response was that he only needed to be genuinely interested in those who he wanted to become long-term profitable clients!

The risk of being perceived as insincere, as disingenuous, as counterfeit or dishonest are some of the critical reasons so many potentially great business winners shy away from anything to do with selling.

CASE STUDY

'David, Thanks so much for the Principled Selling workshop last week. Thought you might like to know that putting into practice what you said about being authentic and genuinely interested in our potential clients has already paid off.

At a meeting with a client we have been trying to win for some time I was very conscious about having the right mindset before the meeting. I was determined to be genuinely interested in the client instead of firing off the usual spiel about our business and how we could help. The meeting went really well and even better I received an e-mail from them saying that it was the first time they had felt a property consultant was really interested in what was best for them – along with a request for a follow up meeting as soon as possible – it works and it's easy now I've stopped trying to "sell"!'

Simon Canning, Head of Facilities Management, London commercial property firm

It is possible that at this stage you will be thinking of customers that right now you would find it difficult to be genuinely interested in. It is possible that you might think it is naïve to believe you can be genuinely interested in all your future prospects. In Chapter 4 you will learn how to guarantee you will only meet with prospects who you do find interesting and whose world you do want to understand.

Principled Selling Tip: Show genuine interest in your customers.

Principle 5 – Being human gets results

We are actors – we're the opposite of people!

Tom Stoppard, Playwright

Over the years I've spent thousands of hours alongside professionals, business owners, technicians and salespeople who seem to change their persona when it's time to sell. It's as though they go from being the normal, friendly, nice person they usually are and transform into some sort of selling machine. They take a deep breath as if steeling themselves for battle, put on their jacket and say things like *Right, let's do it!* Some sales teams even have their morning mantra to get the adrenalin going so that they are ready for anything that their prospects throw at them! Sales training companies, books on selling and motivational sales speakers can have you believing that their particular magic bullet technique or special mental preparation is what you need to succeed in the field.

Selling is not about warfare or for some hugely dangerous expedition where massive reserves of physical and mental energy are needed. Usually the most energetic thing that needs to be done is press the call button for the lift and then sit on a comfortable chair in an air-conditioned meeting room with nice people having a chat about business over a coffee!

Speak with a communications expert like Robin Kermode, an ex-Royal Shakespeare Actor who coaches leading business people and politicians, and he will tell you that as soon as you take a deep breath as if making ready for battle there is a physiological effect. That breath is taken into the top of the lungs and the neck muscles tighten. The body tenses and any verbal and body language communication that follows will either make you appear under-confident or, because some people over-compensate, appear superior or arrogant.

Nerves can get the better of you no matter how experienced you are when you feel uncomfortable about going into a situation that you don't want to be in, in this case a selling situation. There will be times when you have watched an amateur drama production or even some television programme when you find yourself thinking that a character is over-acting, more like a pantomime character than a real human. It doesn't feel right, there is a lack of congruence with the words, tone and body language and it doesn't look real; it looks like an act.

Life is not a stage and we are not all merely actors!

The best actors are those you believe; you trust that they are perfectly in character. It takes years of training to achieve that level of perfection. We recognize when another person is putting on an act and it changes the dynamics of a conversation and whether it is perceived as under-confidence or arrogance it results in reduced belief and trust. If you lack confidence in yourself, your product, service or company it will inevitably lead to a customer's lack of confidence in you.

'It's about having equal status,' says Robin, 'and showing your humanity, never talking down to other people but also never putting other people on a pedestal because it changes the dynamics of a conversation and the way you are perceived. I speak with senior politicians just as I would speak with five-year-old children.' He doesn't mean that politicians need to be spoken down to like some adults might speak to five-years-olds; he means that he speaks with everyone as Robin the human being who happens to be an expert in communication. That is, by not talking down to children and not talking up to senior politicians.

It feels uncomfortable to be with someone who does not behave in a way that reflects equal status. People only buy from people they feel comfortable with.

It's important to accept the fact that other people are as much individuals as you yourself are. They perversely insist on behaving like human beings. This means that they too have their strengths; they too have their ways of getting things done; they too have their values... Each works his or her way, not your way. And each is entitled to work his or her way.

Peter F Drucker, the father of modern management

The best salespeople do not try to force their will on prospects or customers. They respect that people are individuals who like to have the freedom to choose and that customers want to be helped, not patronized. If you are with a person who is overfriendly too early in a relationship it is likely to raise concerns about their motives, you wonder about their real agenda. If you are with someone who goes into pitch mode too soon you are likely to feel that you are being pushed to do something the other person wants rather than being allowed your own freedom to choose. Decision makers rarely say anything if they feel patronized or pressurized, they tend to think *who is this person to speak to me like this* and then they vote with their wallets.

If you make the mistake of putting on your 'selling hat' and attempt to change from your normal personality into a different person, your discomfort when in that false character will show. I have met hundreds of full-time salespeople, professionals and business people who are different characters when they are with their colleagues and family to how they are with customers. That change in character comes about often because of pressure to achieve results, pressure to sell products or services they do not believe in or because they believe that there is a salesperson persona that they think they need to conform to.

Principled Selling Tip: Treat others as equals and allow them to make their own choices.

Selling isn't an innate quality that some people who are born with the 'right' personality have; it is a process and a set of skills and behaviours that can be learned and developed.

In Chapter 3 you will learn about the Principled Selling Growth Model, a tool you can use to help you manage sales growth.

Summary

The five Principles bring Principled Selling to life and when practised together help you to sell ethically, with integrity and with a conscience. Selling is nothing more than the exchange of goods and services for money and when people are motivated to buy, selling is easy. Selling is only uncomfortable when manipulation, persuading or convincing is involved. Long-term profitable relationships depend on trust and today you need to build trust before can earn the right to tell your story. When you have earned the right by investing in a relationship, then feel free to be as passionate and enthusiastic about telling your story as you like! If presenting with passion isn't the real you, don't act; be authentic and be human. Treat others as equals and allow them to make their own choices.

Action points

- Review your own and your team's definition of selling to ensure you are not using words like 'persuade' or 'convince'.
- Check to see if there are any important relationships you should be investing in today.
- Review your business development activity – are you building relationships and earning the right to tell your story?
- Visit **www.principledgroup.com** to download a reminder of the five principles.

PART TWO
PRINCIPLED SELLING IN ACTION

Principled Selling starts with the right mindset and comes alive when you use the tools, skills and behaviours in this section.

Whether your objective is to win more new business, secure existing relationships or win more business from existing customers, in this section you will find all the information you need to make Principled Selling work for you and your organization.

CHAPTER 3

THE PRINCIPLED SELLING GROWTH MODEL

When I look into the future it is so bright it burns my eyes.

Oprah Winfrey

Chapter 2 introduced the five Principles that will help establish the mindset essential to making the processes, skills and behaviours of Principled Selling work for you. This chapter and those following will guide you through the practical application of the Principled Selling Growth Model – the most effective way to guarantee that you win new business, lock in current clients and develop new revenue opportunities with them.

When you implement the Principled Selling Growth Model it makes it easy to apply the five Principles. You identify the prospects that would make ideal customers for your business, develop a deep understanding of how you can help them and provide solutions that deliver on the promises you make. Customers remain loyal because of the service you provide and opportunities for more business are created because you have relationships built on trust.

Success for Principled Sellers depends on understanding the entire business development process and the part that you and others play. Winning more business is much easier when your sales and marketing functions are truly integrated.

The days when the marketing and sales departments lived separate business lives are well and truly over.

Topics covered in this chapter

- Project managing sales growth
- Potential marketplaces and customers
- Begin with the end in mind
- The future state of your business

Project managing sales growth

It is not unusual for sales forecasts to be based simply on adding a percentage increase to a previous period and then hoping for the best. However, your sales revenue to date is the result of marketing activity from months or even years ago and it is not a good indicator of whether future sales forecasts will be met. If you are under your sales budget today, no amount of poring over financial reports is going to help. If you want revenue growth, simply adding a percentage increase based on past results is not much more than a guess or a wish.

Don't get me wrong, financial reports and budgets are really important. Finances must be measured and monitored to ensure a healthy business, but they only provide a historic perspective. The financial results you and your company have achieved up to this moment can't be changed; they are what they are. Using historic financial information to build future revenue forecasts is not the best way forward if you want to be confident about achieving sales growth. It is 'rowing boat management' – looking back to get a perspective on how the future might look, with the odd glance over your shoulder in the hope of avoiding anything that might sink you.

To be confident about future revenue and growth, you need to focus on planning, measuring, monitoring and implementing your sales and marketing activity. You can't change your results to date but you can change the sales and marketing actions you will take today, tomorrow, next week and next month that will ensure you do meet your revenue targets. You need to have enough activity designed to generate enough opportunities to generate enough income.

When you are disciplined and adopt a project-managed approach to selling, your business life becomes easier. You will have a constant flow of opportunities and you will sleep better!

The Principled Selling Growth Model

FIGURE 3.1   Growth model

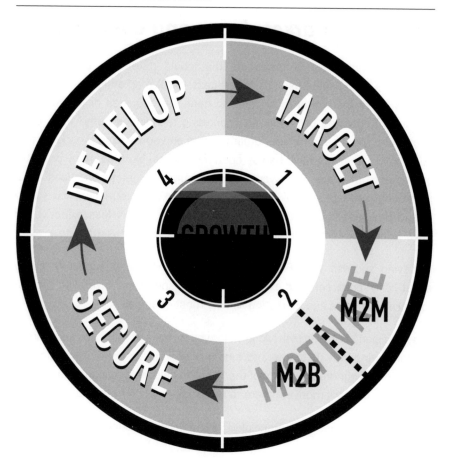

The Principled Selling Growth Model helps you to manage your complete sales process and marketing activity, providing more certainty about achieving the sales growth you want.

The model provides you with a tool to assist you in identifying the most productive areas for you and your team to take action on, whether you need to attract new customers, lock in existing clients or win more business from existing customers.

It is a simple yet highly effective project management tool and you can apply the model whether you want to grow an existing business, start a new business, launch a new product or open an office in a new geographical territory. You can use it to plan and monitor the activity needed to sell to new clients, the activity needed to keep customers loyal and the activity needed to create new opportunities with existing clients.

Potential marketplaces and customers

There are thousands of prospects that could potentially become your customers. Traditional business-to-business (B2B) marketing has tended to employ mass marketing techniques to generate enquiries or leads. Some enquiries generated by traditional marketing techniques come from prospects who could become your dream clients and some from prospects that you would rather not have had as customers at all! With so many potential customers out there, you would need a huge budget to broadcast your marketing messages to all of them. Mass marketing is really most suited to the business-to-consumer (B2C) marketplace and is less effective for developing long-term relationships in business-to-business markets.

Achieving success with Principled Selling depends on being fussy. Fussy about which prospects and existing clients you spend your time with in order to make your sales and marketing activity most effective.

The Principled Selling Growth Model helps you to manage your sales and marketing activity in a way that generates high-quality enquiries from prospects who will become your dream clients of the future. It helps you manage the marketing activity that will motivate them to meet you and buy from you.

There are four stages in the Principled Selling Growth Model: Target, Motivate, Secure, Develop.

Stage 1 – Target

Generating the right type of enquiry is about focus, targeting your sales and marketing activities towards building relationships with:

- market sectors;
- named prospects; and
- specific contacts.

Market sectors

If you are already in business, then you will be trading with market sectors where you already have relationships and where your brand has a reputation. If you are confident that your brand reputation and existing relationships provide enough potential for you to grow profitable sales revenues with the right profile of customer, then your marketing efforts should be focused on those markets and customers you know well.

If you need to broaden your horizons, then your marketing activity will need to focus on building relationships with new sectors.

Many companies for instance have found that in the past the public sector has provided them with enough business to ensure revenue and profit targets were met. Throughout Europe and the USA, for example, budgets in many government departments have been dramatically reduced, with lots of projects cancelled or suspended. If what has been a profitable government department for you is no longer a viable customer, you may have to switch your focus to government departments that are still investing or target the private sector, where you will be unknown.

Targeting the sectors that will provide you with future dream clients allows you to develop a deep understanding about the issues facing your potential customers. When you have that level of understanding you can produce marketing tools and activities which will be relevant and valuable to them. When your marketing activity is focused, relevant and valuable you will generate an increased level of high-quality enquiries.

Named prospects

Named prospects are specific companies or organizations that you believe could become a dream client. You might already have in mind a particular organization that you would really like to do business with; maybe a prestigious name or a company with the potential to provide enough business for you to rapidly expand your own company.

Focusing your marketing activity to build the reputation of your brand in a particular sector might be all that you need to do to provide you with enough high-quality enquiries. If you want to increase the chances of attracting a particular named prospect – a major potential customer for instance – you can target your marketing to zero in on specific organizations. It takes a bit more effort but increases the effectiveness of your marketing.

Specific contacts

If you focus your marketing with laser-like precision you can build relationships with specific contacts in your named prospects. Building one-to-one relationships takes more thought and effort and can only usually be concentrated on a small number of potential dream clients. If they are the type of client that could become very important to the future of your business, then it will be worth the effort.

Stage 2 – Motivate

Once you are clear about your target, then you use your marketing tools and activities to motivate potential customers to make an enquiry about your products and services. When you target your marketing tools and activities on the sectors, named prospects and specific contacts you want to do business with, you will generate the quality of enquiry you need.

Stage 2 of the Growth Model is divided into two segments. 'M2M' is the Principled Selling shorthand for motivating-to-meet. It is marketing activity designed to motivate prospects to meet with you. 'M2B' is shorthand for motivating-to-buy. It includes all the sales and marketing activity involved from a first meeting onwards that motivates a prospect to become a buying customer.

Motivating to meet

M2M marketing involves investment in building relationships by making your marketing tools and activities relevant and valuable to your target market.

CASE STUDY

'We have always had great reputation in the public sector. We knew our skills and knowledge were transferable to private sector organizations and that there was a growing market for our services there but we had no track record or reputation. We applied the thinking behind the Principled Selling Growth Model to our business and started by deciding what the future state of our business should look like. We identified what type of private sector organizations we wanted to target our marketing activity on and invested in developing relevant and valuable content for them. Our M2M efforts started to work almost straight away – we suddenly started getting enquiries from exactly the sort of private sector prospect that we would love to work with. We have already held several meetings and won our first pieces of work. I'm delighted by the progress we have already made by applying the Growth Model.'

David James, Managing Director, Ascentor, Information Risk Consultants

When you are prepared to invest in building relationships before a specific opportunity arises you are demonstrating to potential customers that you are genuinely interested in doing business with them when the time is right. You are demonstrating that you have their interests in mind because you are interested in them before they are in a buying situation. When your interest in the prospect is authentic and you are investing in the relationship before there is a specific opportunity, you build trust in you and your brand.

It might seem that the most opportune time to meet with a potential dream customer is when they are already in the market for what you sell. The downside of trying to build a relationship when a prospect has already decided to seek proposals is that you might be one of several suppliers they will be considering. You might attract their attention through your marketing activity but won't have established relationships. It's why in some sectors when a company goes out to tender the incumbent supplier often wins – because they have an established relationship based on mutual trust.

FIGURE 3.2   The relationship gap

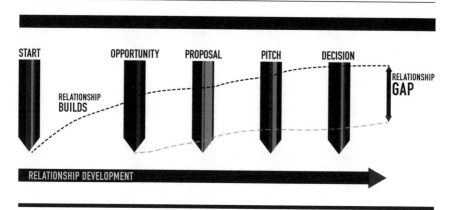

On the right-hand side of the diagram above you will see the typical stages that you might expect in a buying process. An opportunity is identified, some type of proposal is required and maybe a pitch takes place before a decision is made to buy. The buying process might take days, weeks or months but usually doesn't start until a long time after a need has been identified.

The top line left to right in the diagram represents a relationship that starts some time before the buying process begins; the bottom line represents a relationship that starts after the buying process is already underway.

A supplier who starts a relationship before the prospect reveals a specific requirement has a significant competitive advantage. They have the chance to gain insight about what really makes the prospect tick.

Company A and Company B are established software suppliers to the engineering sector. Company A has identified Enstell LLC, a global engineering consultancy, as a potential dream client. As well as focusing their marketing activity on the engineering sector in order to build their reputation they also decided to be proactive and direct some of their marketing resources on developing relationships with Enstell and specific executives of the company, before there was any specific opportunity. When Enstell decided that they needed someone to develop a new project management system they invited Companies A and B to provide proposals. Company B had a good reputation as a supplier to the sector but was unknown to Enstell until after the buying process has started. Both suppliers get the chance to put their solution forward but Company A has a competitive advantage because of their longer-term relationship and the insight they have gained about what makes Enstell 'tick'.

Motivating to buy

There are usually several steps between receiving an enquiry and converting that enquiry into a sale. Typical steps are:

- first sight of the opportunity (enquiry or referral);
- developing a proposal (meetings, written proposal);
- pitching your solution;
- buying decision is made.

As there is inevitably a time lag between each step, it is important to ensure the motivation of the prospect throughout. If you maintain enthusiasm there is never a need to close a sale; the decision to buy from you will be the most natural step for your prospect to take.

Motivating a prospect through the buying process requires an understanding of the selling skills and behaviours that build trust-based relationships.

Stage 3 – Secure

Once a prospect becomes a buying customer, locking them in involves securing the relationship from competitive incursion and maintaining trust so that clients remain loyal. You have to manage your customers' experience so that the service delivered by you and your colleagues is exactly as promised in your sales and marketing messages.

It also involves segmenting your client base in order to decide which customers are key accounts so that you can write an account action plan for them. In Chapter 10 I will show you how to write an account plan that you can use in your business.

Repeat business from loyal customers and clients provides an income stream that is reliable and that you can depend on.

Your business will grow if you provide products that don't come back to customers who do!

Stage 4 – Develop

Even providing great customer service will not guarantee that a client will buy the full range of services you can offer or that you will automatically be invited to supply a different part of their business.

Creating new opportunities with a current client needs planning and a strategy. It calls for relationships to be mapped and understood, new relationships to be built and new marketing campaigns to build trust with new contacts. Cross-selling successfully requires internal strategies to encourage trust, teamwork and cooperation.

A key client account plan should be about *action*, not about recording information about a client. Even for the largest clients an action plan only needs to be three or four pages long.

The model provides a virtuous circle. To win more business you always start with the **Target** stage. Creating new opportunities from current clients, for instance, involves identifying opportunities at the **Develop** stage and then you **Target** individual contacts to build relationships with so that you can **Motivate** them to meet with you and buy from you.

What to measure and monitor

There are many intangibles involved in winning business, such as the strength of customer relationships and the ability to build trust or 'connect' with people.

Sometimes quantitative measurements seem to be too difficult to design. While it is certainly true that there are skills and behaviours to factor in, my experience is that systematically and effectively measuring and monitoring marketing and sales activity is the differentiator between those who *know* what they should do and those who *do* what they should do.

Even some of those things that seem intangible can be measured and monitored. Client relationships can be objectively mapped and measured; selling skills and behaviours can be monitored.

You can bring objective measurements to:

- the number and quality of prospects;
- your marketing activity;
- the number of selling meetings;
- actions that secure loyalty of current clients;
- activity to develop more opportunities;
- the number of client review meetings.

There are many brilliant companies and individuals who fail to achieve their business potential, not because they lack talent, but because they didn't take action. When you set targets for sales and marketing activity you then need to monitor that the targets are being achieved. Activity to generate enquiries will lead to meetings which lead to proposals, presentations, pitches or demonstrations which ultimately lead to sales!

Begin with the end in mind

In the bestselling book *The Seven Habits of Highly Effective People* by Dr Stephen Covey, the first habit is 'begin with the end in mind'. The starting point for any plan, whether it be your life plan or your plan to increase sales has to be to know where you are headed. Once you know what your destination is you can design the strategy that will get you there.

If you don't know where you are going, any road will get you there.

Lewis Carroll

Developing a vision for a business is pretty much standard business practice. A company vision tends to paint a picture of your overall objective as a business. It is an important strategic tool. You can develop a vision for an organization, a geographical territory, a profit centre, a team or even an individual. If you are starting with a complete blank canvas it is probably a little easier than if you have past performance and existing clients to consider. It is possible that you will have inherited someone else's vision of the future or that the vision has been cascaded down through the business. Even if that is the case you can still develop your own vision, which forms part of the greater plan in order that you can play your part in its achievement.

The future state of your business

If you have a trading history you will already know the state of your business as it stands today. You will know your current customer mix, industry sector mix, revenue and margins for each, and your product or service offering for each. You will also understand your current capability to sell new and existing products to new customers as well as new and existing products to current customers.

You can bring the Growth Model to life by having a clear idea of the future state of your own business; for instance where you would like to be in two or three years' time?

If you haven't already written down what the future state of your business looks like, you can start the process by sending yourself an e-mail from the future. Fast-forward three years and imagine you are describing your business in an e-mail to a friend. What does this future message say about:

- the market sectors you are selling to;
- the geographical territories you are selling into;
- the products or services you are providing;
- the number of customers or clients you have;
- the number of key accounts you have;
- the level of fees or price you are charging;
- the gross margins you are achieving;
- the revenue or fee incomes you are achieving;

- the percentage of your revenue being generated from new customers;
- the percentage of your revenue being generated from existing clients.

Even if others proscribe some of the answers, you should still be totally clear in your own mind where you are heading. When you know your destination you can plan the actions that will get you there.

FIGURE 3.3 E-mail from the future

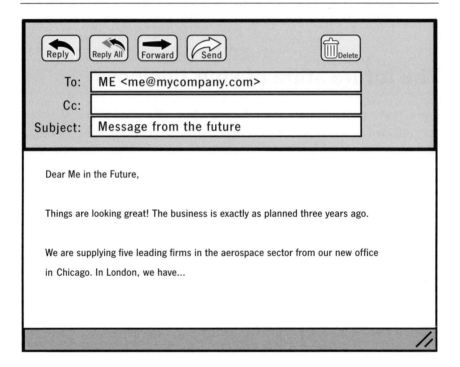

Focusing your resources

Wherever you are right now in terms of generating business you can use the model to work out where you should be focusing your effort for maximum effectiveness.

The Growth Model is presented here as four equal quadrants. In real life the amount of effort invested by an organization isn't distributed so evenly. When you consider the current state of your business what is the proportion of energy devoted to the four Stages? Should it be different in future?

Summary

Measuring past financial performance provides a poor indicator of future sales growth. This month's sales are a result of sales and marketing activity from weeks, months or even years ago. The results you achieve in the future have a direct correlation to the amount of marketing and sales activity you get involved in tomorrow, next week and next month. You can't influence past results but you can massively influence the future by implementing the Principled Selling Growth Model. When you focus your sales and marketing effort on motivating the right prospects to meet you and then motivating them to buy, you will win more business.

Action points

- Review what is measured and monitored in your company. What is talked about most – past results or future business development activity?

- Review how sales targets are set in your company. If necessary ask a key person to confirm the extent to which past sales performance was simply extrapolated to set the new target figures.

- Write an e-mail from the future and set out the future state of your business three years from now.

- Considering the current state of your business, what is the proportion of energy devoted to the four stages of the Growth Model: Target, Motivate, Secure, Develop?

- Consider how your effort should be invested in each of the four Stages to achieve your future state objectives.

- Review how your sales and marketing departments are structured to make sure they are working closely together.

- Visit **www.principledgroup.com/resources**, where you can download an interactive version of the Principled Selling Growth Model.

CHAPTER 4

BRINGING THE GROWTH MODEL TO LIFE

The successful warrior is the average person with a laser-like focus.

Bruce Lee

Chapter 3 introduced the Principled Selling Growth Model. You are now on your journey towards increased sales and ready to bring the Growth Model to life for your business.

To make a start, you need to know which market sectors, which named prospects and which specific contacts you will target, and then focus your M2M (motivate to meet) marketing resources in their direction.

Topics covered in this chapter

- Focusing resources
- Focus on market sector
- Selecting named prospects
- Stage 1 target research

Focusing resources

Winning more business isn't like fighting a battle with winners and losers. The best salespeople don't think of themselves as warriors; however there is a lot that can be learned from successful military strategies.

When Sun Tzu wrote about focus of forces in *The Art of War* (around 500 BC) he established two winning military tactics: gather good intelligence and concentrate overwhelming firepower on enemy positions. For thousands of years that meant having superior numbers of soldiers, but that has now been refined to mean more effective and better resourced forces. Rather than overrun a position with huge numbers of troops, today intelligence provides detailed information on targets so that 'smart' munitions can be delivered with incredible accuracy. Large armies are no longer needed; modern technology allows even the smallest of forces to be highly effective.

Mass marketing and broadcasting your message far and wide is the equivalent of putting faith in superior numbers. M2M marketing is smart marketing – using modern marketing methods and technology to focus your messages where your research suggests they will be most effective and win most business.

Focus on market sectors

Building long-term profitable relationships depends on potential customers feeling you understand their world. That is much easier to achieve if you focus on niche markets that you are interested in and that you are knowledgeable about. It is also easier for you and your brand to be famous and for your company to become the 'go to' supplier.

Becoming a 'go to' supplier is possible whatever your product or service. Niche markets work as well for freelance management consultants as they do for fee earners in a professional practice, technology vendors selling CRM systems or aerospace companies selling jet engines.

Deciding on market sectors depends a great deal on how comfortable you are about being able to deliver on your sales and marketing messages. You might be aware that a particular market sector is buoyant right now and that there are exciting opportunities for the product or service you provide. When focusing your efforts there you have to be sure that you will be as good at delivery and execution as you are at sales and marketing.

Ask yourself and your colleagues:

- Why is this sector attractive to us?
- Do we understand the sector?
- Do we have the right products and services?
- Will our products or services need any modification?
- Do we have the resources to service customers in the sector?
- Can we deliver on our promises?

CASE STUDY

'As a Sunday Times Top 100 Company to Work For, we have worked hard to build our brand and to become trusted advisors to our customers. A couple of years ago we found that our reputation was attracting regular enquiries for CRM systems from a new market sector that we hadn't supplied before but that we felt offered significant opportunities. Our first thought was to find out if we really understood the market and if we would need to make any changes to our usual technical solutions. Feedback from the sales, installation and technical support teams was that we didn't have the depth of knowledge we would need to deliver to the levels of excellence our customers were used to. We decided to recruit the expertise required and get the new recruits familiar with our high service culture before we were happy to take our first orders. Now we are the leading provider of CRM systems in that market.'

Mike Bentley, Sales Director, JMC IT Ltd

If you are a freelance consultant or in professional practice you might decide to focus your sales and marketing effort on one sector where you know you can make a real impact. If you are part of a team you might be able to target several sectors. The best recruitment consultancies for example have 'desks'. Each desk consists of a team of people who live and breathe a particular market sector which they understand and build relationships with. If a desk special-izes in recruiting Mergers and Acquisition Specialists in the financial services sector, all their intelligence gathering and sales and marketing activity is focused on that market.

Be clear about the market sectors that you want to become famous in and you will know where to target your sales and marketing activity.

Selecting named prospects

Employing a simple selection criteria tool will help you to identify where your sales activity should be focused. Target selection criteria will be different depending on your industry, the product or service you sell and your business objectives.

The criteria you use for selecting named prospects should be based on the factors that make a sector or individual client more attractive for you to approach. The most sensible place to start is to think about your best current clients. Capture all the criteria that make them your ideal customers. If you are starting with a blank sheet go back to your thinking around designing your future state and what an ideal client might look like in three years' time. Another way to think about it is if the phone rang today and it was your perfect client calling, what criterion makes them a perfect client?

Parameters you employ in your Stage 1 Target might include:

- revenue potential;
- profit potential;
- growth potential;
- number of people employed;
- type of work you want to do;
- geographical locations of the client match your own;
- your expertise in the sector;
- your ability to effectively service the sector or client;
- your service or product is in demand or of particular benefit;
- strategic importance of a specific client;
- ethics or morals of a potential client;
- type of relationship you want.

Examples of Stage 1 Target client selection criteria are shown in the box.

Freelance marketing consultant

My dream clients are:

- private companies with 50+ employees;
- companies where the owners and/or managers will value the creativity I bring to marketing;
- owners and/or managers who want a trusted advisor relationship;
- companies where I can add real value and make a difference;
- companies with potential for repeat work;
- customers who pay on time.

Commercial property consultant

Our dream clients are:

- private or public sector organizations with a national property portfolio;
- organizations with potential for cross-selling our full range of services;
- organizations with office locations that match ours;
- organizations where we have a track record in the sector;
- organizations investing in growth;
- organizations that fit with our corporate strategy.

Software vendor

Our dream customers are:

- in the aerospace industry;
- high-profile names;
- pioneers or early adopters;
- organizations with a minimum IT budget of $2 million;
- current users of ERP systems;
- prepared to help with development;
- organizations with a partnership attitude;
- socially aware;
- in the USA.

Engineering consultancy

Our dream clients are:

- in the energy sector;
- seeking long-term relationships;
- involved in projects where we have specialized expertise;
- involved in projects where we have a good track record;
- organizations where we have named contacts;
- a good cultural fit with our business;
- organizations where there will be no conflict of interests for us.

You can use the same approach if you are launching a new product or service. Establish selection criteria based on what type of client or customer would be more attractive and easier to approach rather than broadcasting marketing messages far and wide in the hope that some will attract enquiries from dream clients.

There can sometimes be a tendency to focus too much on financial or other objective criteria, ie what you will get as a result of winning an ideal client. These may be important, but other more subjective criteria like cultural fit and strategic importance should also be thought about.

It might be that if you win a big player in a particular sector that this will establish your credibility with other organizations in the same market. Even if one of your criteria might be a minimum level of business potential, you may be willing to do a smaller amount of business with a major player if it contributes to your brand being placed firmly on the map as a trusted provider to that sector. You or your colleagues may even already know by name a number of prospects that you would love to have as clients because of who they are.

With your team, identify up to eight criteria for your business.

TABLE 4.1   My named prospect selection criteria

1	
2	
3	
4	
5	
6	
7	
8	

The selection criteria you choose will help you to build a database of target markets and individual clients that you will proactively market to. Remember that to include also means to exclude. Be disciplined about selecting the sectors and individual clients you will target because you will be focusing all your sales and marketing efforts into winning business there.

The number of prospects you will need on your database will depend on your particular business. The key is to have the number of targets that you can pro-actively manage. For a partner in an accountancy firm this might mean having no more than 10 named prospects at any one time to be building relationships with. If you are selling full time you might be able to cope with significantly more.

Stage 1 target research

Your target market will want to know that you really understand their world. That understanding starts with what you read. If you are reading magazines, periodicals and web portals about your own industry, then you are focusing on your own world rather than your clients'. Your own industry media will supply you with news, information and gossip about your own business environment. What you really need is news, information and gossip about your customers' business environment. When you read what your clients read you start to build insight into what makes them and their industry tick. This information will be invaluable to you throughout your M2M and M2B activities.

Take a look right now around your offices and in your reception area. What magazines do you see – are they the same ones your clients read? Check your browser for your favourite sites. Have you bookmarked the sites that your target market visits to stay informed? Are they the same one's your prospects and clients read? If they are, great! If not, then maybe you should think about taking out some new subscriptions and logging on to some new websites.

CASE STUDY

'I'm an accountant by training but haven't read anything that comes from the accountancy press for years. I specialize in the franchise industry, so I absorb myself in everything franchise related. I read franchising blogs and network on and offline with people involved in franchising. My clients expect me to be able to deliver accountancy services. It says my firm are accountants on my business card. That is not a differentiator. The differentiator is when they know that I understand them and the franchising industry, that I speak their language. That makes it easy to buy from me and it's why we have so many franchiser and franchisee clients.'

Carl Reader, Partner, Dennis and Turnbull, Accountants

You only need enough information to start your M2M marketing activities, so don't go overboard with your research!

Researching named prospects

Keeping yourself informed about what is going on in the target market(s) you have chosen is a great starting point. Simply keeping up-to-date with what is going on will present you with names of potential prospects you may not have known existed and information on events happening in the sector that might generate interest in your product or service.

When you target named prospects your intelligence-gathering activity will need to be a bit more specific. Having information about the energy industry is one thing, having information on one company such as a global business like Halliburton is another. Being sure exactly which named prospect you are targeting is also an important decision to make. If Halliburton made it onto your dream client list do you target their Drilling and Evaluation Division or their Completion and Production Division? Do you target their North American or International operations and which of their five brands do you target? Companies like Halliburton, Virgin, BP, Vodafone, GE or Astra Zeneca are huge organizations with multiple subsidiaries and divisions. All these companies do business with thousands of suppliers. If you want them as a customer or client it starts with knowing where you will target your M2M marketing!

You can gain intelligence on your named prospects from:

- their website;
- their blog (if they host one);
- their LinkedIn profile(s);
- their Twitter timeline;
- their profile on Facebook;
- industry press;
- associations they may be members of;
- networking events;
- industry conferences.

You are not seeking to build a huge intelligence file on your named prospects. The information you gather will help you decide if they meet your selection criteria and how to market to them.

Basic information for a named prospect in Stage 1 Target:

- Name and address details
- Telephone number
- Website address
- Company LinkedIn profile
- Company Facebook profile
- Company Twitter profile.

You can use the company profiles to identify specific contacts, their roles and areas of expertise.

Researching specific contacts

Imagine that you have decided to target the Energy sector and you have selected Halliburtons' Sperry Drilling company in North America as your named prospect. Next you need to research who the actual decision makers and influencers are. A business doesn't build a relationship with another business. People build relationships with people.

Building relationships with people who can influence decisions is as important as building relationships with decision makers because it is rare for buying decisions to made by one individual in isolation, no matter what their level of seniority. While there are few people who have the authority to say *yes* to you, there are plenty of people who can give you a *no* by blocking your proposals or favouring other suppliers. You might need to build relationships across several departments in some larger companies. Fortunately modern technology makes it easier than ever to build relationships at all levels within your target prospect.

In some sectors and in some organizations it might be a procurement department or buyer in a particular area of the business who normally purchases your type of product or service. Even when that is the case don't be afraid to develop relationships at as senior a level as possible. Senior executives have discretionary budgets, while most other managers have fixed budgets. You will need to be able to deliver the right messages to senior executives, but for now you should concentrate on finding out who they are.

CASE STUDY

'Typically most organizations will have a designated individual who deals with information security matters. They know what they are doing and take their role very seriously but can sometimes be a lone voice in recognizing the importance of information security. For many, the process has therefore become a tick box exercise doing just enough to gain an accreditation. We knew information security should be a strategic issue for CEOs, so we identified the senior executives we wanted to influence and set to work building relationships with them. Now we have information security being talked about around the boardroom table!'

David James, Managing Director, Ascentor, Information Risk Consultants

Involve your colleagues in your research and you might be surprised how many of them will have knowledge of the named prospect you are targeting. Your colleagues might have worked with them in the past, might know people there or might know someone who does. Intelligence gathered in this way can be worth its weight in gold; it might even be intelligence that is exclusively yours, as your competitors only know at best what is in the public domain.

Influence and perception

If you are targeting a really important prospect, the type of prospect that, if you win their business, could make a serious contribution to the growth of your company, then there is one more level of research you should consider. When you have your list of key influencers and decision makers, communicate again with colleagues to find out as much as you can about: each contact's ability to influence the decision to buy from you; and each contact's perception of you and your brand, product or services.

It might be that you can answer both questions for all contacts but it is likely that there will be gaps in your knowledge. That's OK. If you are targeting a key prospect, knowing and understanding the gaps in your knowledge will help you with your marketing strategy later.

For an important named prospect your analysis might look like this:

TABLE 4.2 Relationship matrix tool

Specific contact	Position	Level of influence	Perception of us
Sarah Hodge	CEO	High	Unknown
Michael Stuart	VP Production	High	High – previous client
Karen Evans	Sales Manager	Unknown	Unknown

When you have this level of intelligence you can use your marketing strategy to develop relationships in a way that no mass marketing activity will ever achieve. You will be able to motivate the right people in the right target prospects to want to meet with you, while most of your competitors continue to simply bombard the same people with mass marketing messages that are never seen.

Summary

Increasing your sales revenue, from clients who buy and re-buy, starts at Stage 1 Target of the Principled Selling Growth Model. While selling should never be thought of as a battle with winners and losers, there is a great deal to be learned from military strategists about focusing resources where they are most likely to be effective. Find the right niche markets where your brand can become famous and where you are comfortable that you will be able to deliver excellent service. When you have niche markets to focus on, develop selection criteria for your dream clients and select named prospects and specific contacts to develop relationships with.

Action points

- Select the market sector(s) where you want to be famous.

- Develop selection criteria for your dream clients.

- Research potential dream clients to collect basic information for your M2M marketing activities.

- Research specific contacts you would like to build relationships with.

- Using the relationship matrix tool, identify influence levels and perception.

If you use the interactive Principled Selling Growth Model you downloaded from the website you can do all the above using the templates provided.

CHAPTER 5

M2M (MOTIVATE TO MEET) MARKETING

The traditional model we all grew up with is obsolete.

Jim Stengel, Global Marketing Officer Procter & Gamble

You now have a clear idea of which market sectors you want to be famous in and have developed selection criteria that will assist you to determine named prospects. You have researched the named prospects you want to build relationships with and have identified specific contacts who can influence or make decisions to buy your products or services.

Now we will explore how to employ M2M (motivate to meet) marketing to generate enquiries and how to motivate senior executives in your future dream client companies to meet with you.

Topics covered in this chapter

- Why traditional marketing isn't working any more
- Building trusted relationships through your marketing
- Using valuable content to motivate prospects to meet you

Why traditional marketing isn't working any more

Challenging times for marketers

At a time when winning more business has become more important than ever, many organizations have looked at how they spend their marketing budgets and how the marketing team is deployed. In a global professional services firm I worked with recently they reduced their client social events costs last year to almost zero by redeploying the people who organized events to other 'more direct marketing' activities. Those other duties involved producing more corporate literature, newsletters, sector brochures and updating their website to be modern and 'punchy'. They also employed an external telemarketing company to generate leads and build their marketing database so that they had more names to send their corporate literature to.

The client was absolutely right to reduce their level of hospitality. Their return on investment didn't justify the costs involved any more, though in previous years it had seemed a worthwhile investment. After a year of increasing their spending on being more direct and punchy they called me in because that didn't seem to be producing much of a return on that investment either!

What's happening?

Tried and tested activities for getting customer attention are just not working like they once did.

Sonja Jefferson, *Valuable Content Marketing*

It has been the age-old marketing challenge – attracting enough enquiries from the right prospects that will result in a conversation about doing business. As Sonja alludes to in her quote above, the challenge has become more challenging!

- The response to cold-calling and direct mail campaigns is massively down.
- The niche press and magazines that you might have once relied on for cost effective marketing, are fast disappearing.
- Advertising is expensive and isn't generating enough enquires to justify the cost.
- Even enquiries from established referral networks are under pressure as all markets become more competitive.

Telemarketing isn't working as well as it once did. In 2006 it took only six calls from a telemarketing firm to make one contact according to Hot to Trot Marketing. By last year that had rocketed to 41. This year and next it will be tougher still.

Mashable, the digital news site, undertook research recently finding that 45 per cent of direct mail is never opened. They also found that 86 per cent of people skip through television commercials and 85 per cent of 25–35 year olds have clicked out of a website because of an 'irrelevant or intrusive ad'.

It's not just 25–35 year olds that get frustrated with irrelevant and badly targeted messages either. In a series of rants on Twitter a bunch of more mature grey-haired Tweeters were bemoaning the number of direct messages they receive asking them to click on links that direct them to special offers. *Stop trying to grab our attention with messages that steal time from us* was pretty much the message. People today not only get frustrated about receiving e-mails into their overloaded inbox from people they don't know, they get frustrated at a 140 character message in their Twitter timeline!

As of February 2012, over 17 million UK phone numbers were registered with the Telephone Preference Service (the 'do not call me' list). In North America, the US Securities and Exchange Commission *Do Not Call Registry* now tops 200 million! That's a lot of people who bothered to register that they definitely don't want to receive sales calls! When a federal judge puts three businesses into receivership and freezes the assets of their owners for infringements of the *Do Not Call Registry* and a major UK domestic insurance company is fined £750,000 for making nuisance calls it might seem enough to put you off marketing altogether.

It no longer makes economic sense to send an advertising message to the many in the hopes of persuading a few.
M Lawrence Light, former Chief Marketing Officer, McDonald's

The old methods have been pushing ever more direct marketing messages at their audience that don't work any more. That's why I was called in by the professional services firm I mentioned above. They thought they needed to be more 'salesy' and more 'punchy' towards more people in order to win more business when what they actually needed was to use their marketing to motivate their potential clients.

Not marketing – motivating!

The best marketing is 'pull' marketing. Like a magnet it attracts your potential clients and customers. Your marketing activities motivate the right people to come to you. They call you instead of you calling them, they want to meet you, and they want to discuss the potential of doing business with you. Forget about marketing and think motivating!

When you think *motivating* instead of *marketing* it helps you focus on what your customer wants to achieve and how you can help them. It is an authentic client-focused way of building relationships and avoids the temptation of ever making claims in marketing messages that cannot be delivered on.

Motivating your target prospects to make enquiries and to meet with you involves activities that will build trust *before* you enter into face-to-face dialogue to discuss opportunities. From now on you will only ever meet decision makers who want to spend time with you, who trust you and who would make ideal clients and customers!

CASE STUDY

'It's fascinating how a simple change of language can completely alter your perspective on something. In a meeting with David Tovey of Principled Selling fame, we were discussing how customers buy and which parts are marketing, which sales, and which customer service.

To my mind, marketing has always been the act of taking your products and services to market, and is therefore the umbrella term for the joined up whole. However, I conceded that most people see marketing as filling the top end of a sales funnel. The awareness and lead generation bit. Then David said something brilliant. He said, "We don't call it marketing; we call it motivating" – and he is spot on!'

Bryony Thomas, business speaker, marketing consultant and author of *Watertight Marketing*

Why trust matters

Making business decisions involves risk. Risk comes in many forms and if you ask any good information risk consultant they will list the zillions of ways a company can be negatively affected by making the wrong decision. Depending on what a customer is buying, the consequences of making the wrong decision can range from minor irritation to extremely serious.

You might think buying photocopier paper carried little risk. On the surface if someone decided to go for a special offer from a new supplier to save money and then the paper that is delivered is poor quality and unusable you could be forgiven for thinking the cost is just that paid for the paper. However there could be more serious consequential losses.

The paper jams the photocopier in the office of the PA to the CEO just when an important document needs copying for a meeting with shareholders. A tender document for a prestigious and valuable contract goes out looking shabby, risking a multimillion-dollar opportunity. Would you want to be explaining why, in your effort to shave a small amount from the stationery budget, you had caused serious embarrassment to the CEO or potentially cost your company millions of dollars? No? Nor would I!

That's why most people buying photocopier paper go to the supplier they trust. The risk of something going wrong is minimal. Even if a 50 per cent discount offer comes in from an unknown supplier, a risk assessment will be made.

The same thinking applies to all sorts of apparently minor decisions. *'When the seafood comes in it's perfect'*, a Chef said to me recently when discussing a supplier. *'It's not worth the risk of going elsewhere to buy just to save money.'*

Risk assessments are being made by us all the time when it comes to buying decisions. It used to be said that no one ever got fired for buying IBM. It is the same reason the FTSE 100 and Fortune 100 companies so often employ 'magic circle' law firms or top-four accountancy firms. Financial Directors and General Counsels know they could get the same quality of legal advice and probably save money by going to the next tier of firms; but they don't. They know there is little or no risk to working with the well-known names in law and accountancy.

Buyers at all levels know that some of their own credibility is on the line when they decide to purchase something for their organization. From minor decisions about stationery supplies to life or death decisions about health and safety equipment, transport systems or nuclear power stations – buyers think about risk.

CASE STUDY

'I've dealt with Grontmij for 25 years. I first worked with them when I was a trainee – now I am responsible for commissioning major infrastructure projects from them across Europe. I trust them, they mean what they say – why would I work with anyone else?'

Danish client, speaking at Grontmij conference in the Netherlands.
(Grontmij are a pan-European engineering group)

Human beings like to have relationships with people they can trust. It's a basic human need. Teams deliver high performance, and personal and business relationships thrive when they are built on trust.

Motivating someone in a target market or named prospect to make an enquiry and to meet you is easier when you build trust through your marketing.

Building trusted relationships through your marketing

You may recall from Chapter 1 that the Edelman Barometer of Trust established that, to get information they trust, people go to:

- people who are similar to them;
- their social networks (online and offline);
- micro-blogging sites (such as Twitter);
- websites which share valuable content.

This is great news for Principled Sellers who use M2M marketing. Your target markets, prospects and contacts will trust your information if they feel you understand their world and their issues, when you are part of their wider network both online and offline and when you provide them with content that they will value. The content they will value is called – valuable content!

Valuable content – what is it?

You can buy attention (advertising)

You can beg for attention from the media (PR)

You can bug people one at a time to get attention (traditional sales)

Or you can earn attention by creating something interesting and valuable and then publishing it...

David Meerman Scott, *New Rules of PR and Marketing*

In the context of M2M marketing, 'content' is the words you read in an article, a book, on a website or in a Tweet. It is the video and images you share, the slides you make available after a presentation. Content simply means words, knowledge and information.

Valuable content is high-performance content. It is high-performance because it has a bigger purpose: to provide useful information for a particular audience. Valuable content is the words, knowledge and information you shape and share with potential clients and customers that they will really appreciate because it is meaningful and right on target.

When you use valuable content in your M2M marketing activity you will start to build relationships within your chosen market sectors, with named prospects and with the specific contacts you have identified.

CASE STUDY

'Today, effective marketing is all about creating high-quality content and sharing it. By quality content we don't just mean information that is well written or artfully produced. By quality content we mean information that is first and foremost of real value to your particular client base.

Educate your clients, show them best practice, tell them what to look out for, give them valuable tips on how to achieve success, demonstrate how you've helped others in their shoes; answer their problems, open their eyes.

Creating and distributing this kind of relevant, valuable and compelling information will help you turn prospects into buyers and buyers into long-term fans.'

Sonja Jefferson, *Valuable Content Marketing*

Too often marketing materials, brochures, websites and advertising are just not meaningful to potential customers and clients. They often boast about the supplier, telling the world how great they are. There is a time to tell a prospect how good you are – but that comes later in the business development process when you have earned the right to boast – not when you are starting out to build relationships.

Traditional marketing is often more about what motivates the seller, not what motivates the potential buyer!

Content that is valuable and works is:

- focused – relevant and meaningful to your target audience;
- useful – it informs, educates and sometimes entertains;
- authentic – it reflects the real you and your company;
- high-quality – interesting, well produced and has substance;
- clear and compelling – it tells a story that is understandable and motivates a response.

CASE STUDY

'Having developed a very good reputation with public sector clients, we wanted to build the same reputation in the private sector where we saw lots of new opportunities. The problem was that we had no private clients. Without an existing network or contacts in this market we wanted a new approach to building our reputation without resorting to traditional mass marketing techniques.

We developed criteria for what would be our ideal private client with the help of our marketing agency and set about developing content our new target market would find valuable. First we had professional copywriters look at our website content and develop pages specifically for the private sector. We developed an online analysis tool and a number of articles. We also produced *The Executive Guide to Information Security* as we really wanted to get the attention of board-level decision makers.

After a couple of months we launched a new social media based website and blog with contributions from every member of our consultancy team and the CEO.

The new approach to valuable content marketing brought immediate results. *The Executive Guide* started to be downloaded from our website in large numbers and we were soon in conversation with private companies. We are right on target for the level of business we wanted to achieve without investing anything in product brochures or advertising.'

David James, Managing Director, Ascentor

Companies succeeding with valuable content marketing right now

Capita Symonds

A 50-office subsidiary of Capita (global provider of business process outsourcing and support service solutions to the defence, health and education sectors), which strengthened relationships with key target clients by focusing on valuable content campaigns.

Intel Corporation

Intel has focused on creating valuable content for each of its different communities. Their blogs, social media feeds, video and even processor 'art' give the company a human face and expand the influence of their messages.

Coca-Cola

Long wedded to creative advertising, Coca-Cola announced in 2012 that it was planning to double its business by switching its focus to sharing excellent content.

IBM

Now famous for their industry sector white papers, which provide thought leadership without being self-promotional and which provide masses of material via their blogs, videos and social media activities.

Accenture

Provides a podcast library of well-researched and targeted educational content (for sectors from chemicals to IT to consulting) which can be delivered straight to their clients and potential clients inboxes.

But you don't have to be a big corporation to succeed with valuable content. Look at the following.

Indium Corp.

A team of 16 engineers who have become famous for bringing highly technical ideas to life through their blog *From one engineer to another* – engineers doing marketing!

Hinge Marketing

A niche marketing agency based in Reston, Virginia, which self-publishes highly targeted books, delivers excellent free webinars and provides helpful tips and information through their monthly newsletter which has made them famous in professional services.

Mel Lester

A US freelance business consultant who shares useful articles and resources via his website blog, Twitter feed and monthly newsletter, which now generates 70 per cent of his new business.

Iain Claridge

A UK web designer whose inspirational design blog landed him work all over the world, including with NASA.

Yoke

A start-up sustainable web design company which had all the clients they needed, plus a waiting list, six weeks after launch, thanks to their content-rich website, compelling proposition and Twitter relationships.

And us!

At Principled Selling our blogs, articles, downloads and even this book are part of the valuable content we continually generate to attract great clients. We have never advertised or used brochures or telemarketing – our M2M campaigns have earned us the right to engage with leading organizations all over the world.

CASE STUDY

'Remember that the prospects you are targeting are as busy, as cynical, as suspicious and as over-sold as you. The only way to stop people hitting the delete button or marking your e-mail as spam or committing your brochure to the waste bin is to provide something that they find interesting and of value.'

Sharon Tanton, *Valuable Content Marketing*

Using valuable content to motivate prospects to meet you

How can valuable content work for you?

Valuable content will reach more potential customers and clients than any brochure, mail shot or e-mail marketing campaign. When you provide content that is meaningful and useful you earn the right to engage with potential customers and clients. Valuable content flies under an organization's anti-marketing radar because it is useful.

From web search to sale

When a potential customer in your target sector has a challenge they want to solve and when you have invested in valuable content marketing, it works like this:

- They search Google for information about their challenge (85 per cent of adults who use the internet do so for finding information).
- Your content has placed your name at the top of page one on search engines.
- They land on an article, e-book or video you have created about the challenge they face.
- They read your content and are impressed with your insight into their world.
- They check your website and see that you specialize in their market sector.
- They sign up for your newsletter, follow your blog and Tweets and connect with you on LinkedIn.
- They also spot your articles in industry magazines or possibly hear you speak at a conference. Their respect for your insight into their world increases.
- They are motivated to contact you to arrange an exploratory meeting – and ultimately motivated to buy from you.

CASE STUDY

Balsamiq is a software company with a hugely popular mock up tool used by web designers all over the world. From day one, founder Giacomo 'Peldi' Guilizzoni blogged openly about his experiences, even giving away details of his revenue figures. Written from the heart his blog built an active community of followers who spread the word. All this goodwill and exposure helped his software go from zero to leader in just six months.

25 examples of valuable content tactics:

- Articles
- White papers
- Blog
- E-newsletter
- E-book
- Case study
- Micro-blogging
- Webinar
- Video
- Community website
- Video blog
- E-learning series
- Mobile applications (apps)

- Teleseminar
- Podcast
- Executive round tables
- Book
- Print newsletter
- Speaker platforms
- Widget
- Branded content tool
- Infographic
- Online survey research project
- Discussion forum
- iPad application

Over time you can build a library of collateral material that you can use to build and maintain trusted relationships with existing customers and prospects. You will learn lots more about valuable content tactics and how technology such as social media can help you in Chapter 6.

Valuable content campaigns

You can meet the senior executives of your dream client companies if you build a valuable content campaign (VCC) just for them. A VCC is based on two or three tailored letters or e-mails sent to a specific contact over several weeks with different interesting and useful content attached. VCCs are highly effective in motivating senior executives to meet you and to help you build a trusted relationship.

A typical VCC works like this:

● Identify the specific contact you want to do business with and do your research.

- Choose three tactics from your valuable content library or create something that your prospect will find useful: an article, an e-book and a white paper for instance.
- Send a tailored letter with the article to your specific contact.
- Seven to 10 days later send a tailored e-mail with a link to your e-book.
- Seven to 10 days later send a tailored letter with a copy of your white paper.
- Craft each letter and e-mail carefully – your aim is to help, not pitch.
- Follow up your campaign with a phone call to make an appointment to meet – your contact will be motivated to take your call – occasionally they will call you first!

You can also use your valuable content to support your VCC:

- Put your article, e-book and white paper on your website.
- Blog about them.
- Tweet about them.
- Share them with your contacts on LinkedIn.
- Feature them in your e-newsletter.
- Put a link to your e-book in your e-mail signature.
- Create a press release about your e-book.
- Submit your article and white paper to industry magazines.

When the senior executive researches who has been sending them useful and interesting material, they will discover your blog, visit your website, follow your Tweets and connect with you on LinkedIn. They will also suggest colleagues do the same. With your support tactics in place you will start to build trusted relationships with a wider group of influencers and decision makers.

Valuable content marketing is sticky marketing. Anything that is interesting and useful has a long shelf life; it stays on your prospect's desk and its stays in their mind. With valuable content you are always in the right place at the right time, top of your prospect's mind, unlike mass marketing, cold-calling brochures or advertising.

CASE STUDY

'We had been trying to get an appointment with the CEO of a subsidiary company in a global technology business famous for smart phones and tablet computers. We knew we had something to offer but we were just a small software developer in a business where there were dozens of people like us wanting to get a meeting. When we learned about valuable content campaigns it made us cringe at our previous attempts. We had even tried an external telesales company. We did the research as advised by the Principled Selling guys and got down to finding and writing content that would be useful to the CEO. We got the opportunity to get involved in some research and we used the results as part of a valuable content campaign. When it came to making the phone call I prepared myself for various obstacles like a PA who would intervene but to my surprise I was put straight through to the CEO and after a short conversation I'd booked an appointment. At the meeting it was like having a chat with someone we'd known for years. Three months later we were doing our first business with them. All because we took time to build a relationship before we tried to tell our own story.'

Ricky Camelleri, VP Marketing, audio software developer, Birmingham

Keep in touch!

Not every valuable content campaign you undertake will lead to a meeting. If your campaign does not result in a meeting in the near future, go back to your Growth Model and make a decision about whether you will keep in touch with the contact or find a new named prospect. If the target remains a dream client continue to keep in touch with valuable content but on a less frequent basis. That way you will be top of their mind when the timing is right.

A word of warning about keeping in touch after a campaign: do *not* simply put the target's contact into a marketing database so that they receive generic marketing messages, newsletters and invitations via post or e-mail. Even if the timing wasn't right, you will have put yourself on the radar of a very important potential customer. Your VCC has provided your named prospect with useful and interesting materials and they will be positive towards you. They may even be looking forward to a time when there is an opportunity to invite you to start a dialogue with them. If you fail to keep in touch at all, their enthusiasm will gradually fade away, you might be forgotten and your competitor might be around to provide enthusiasm at the right time. Keeping in touch with generic marketing information will drive your contact away very quickly.

Principled Selling Tip: Keep in touch on a less frequent basis but still using valuable content that is relevant, interesting and useful to your prospect.

Dealing with unexpected enquiries

Designing your future involves proactively managing all your business development activities. Motivating specific named prospects to meet with you is a key element of your strategy. Nevertheless, your marketing activity will also generate enquiries from organizations not included in your target list of dream customers and this has the potential to send you off course unless you have an objective way of dealing with them.

When an unexpected enquiry comes in, all too often salespeople fall over themselves to get hold of the lead. After all, that must mean the enquiry is probably from someone who is in the market for your products or services. That might be right but the risk is that you will chase leads that could result in selling to entirely wrong clients.

The answer is to create criteria for unexpected enquiries as you did for your named prospects. A shortlist of five or six criteria will help you decide if the enquiry is one that you should actively pursue. It's the same principle that you probably already apply to dealing with invitations to tender to help you decide whether it's a bid/no bid situation.

If the enquiry matches your established criteria, then by all means put into practice what you have learned and motivate the decision maker to meet with you!

Summary

Traditional marketing just isn't working any more. Cold-calling, advertising, direct mail, e-mail marketing and even social media can infuriate people these days. With an audience more cynical than ever about marketing techniques that 'push' messages, smart companies use M2M marketing to attract enquiries from their target markets and generate meetings with dream clients. Making decisions about what to buy and who to buy from involves risk and buyers reduce the risk of consequential loss by dealing with people they trust. You can start to build trust with your target markets and named prospects by implementing M2M marketing, which uses valuable content to attract enquiries and generate meetings with senior executives. Valuable content provides interesting and useful information that named prospects find relevant and meaningful.

Action points

- Review your marketing approach – do you depend too much on the old tried and tested techniques that push your sales messages?
- Review your marketing material to see if they match the definition of valuable content.
- Meet with your team and generate ideas for valuable content that would be useful and interesting to your target market and named prospects.
- Start to build a library of valuable content collateral.
- Select a named prospect that you would like to win business from and create a valuable content campaign.
- Downloaded the Principled Selling Growth Model – use the templates and tools to help you develop your M2M marketing activity. **www.principledgroup.com/resources**

CHAPTER 6

WINNING MORE BUSINESS WITH NETWORKING AND SOCIAL MEDIA

How can you squander even one more day not taking advantage of the greatest shifts of our generation? How dare you settle for less when the world has made it so easy for you to be remarkable?

Seth Godin

The previous chapter introduced M2M (motivate to meet) marketing, the most powerful way you can engage with your target market, named prospects and specific contacts. With valuable content at the heart of your marketing you are ready to start building trusted relationships and bring your marketing right up to date using the power of online and offline networking.

Topics covered in this chapter

- The serious business of social networking
- How social media engages your prospects and clients
- Social media tools and how to use them
- The Principled Selling Approach to social media
- A guide to offline networking

The serious business of social networking

All major brands across the world are interacting with their customers and potential customers using social media. In both business-to-consumer and business-to-business communication, social media has become an important tool for people serious about marketing. The great news is that the benefits can be achieved whatever the size of your organization. Even individuals are making themselves and their brand famous online in weeks and months these days – it doesn't take years to establish yourself as the Go To person any more!

Social media

Business use of social media is not about banal or trivial chat, it is not a fad and it is not about geeky technology. It is a serious business tool and, as you read in Chapter 1, its use is growing at an incredible rate. It is no more about technology than using your smart phone or driving your car is – both complex technical products that you learn to use for the benefits they give you.

Social media is the term used to identify the various platforms that provide you with the opportunity to undertake *social networking.* Sadly social networking is a term that many businesses misinterpret as something employees should only do out of working hours. Some organizations misunderstand social networking in business so much that they ban their employees from using it and even spend money on technology to bar access to social networking sites. In the context of winning more business it is no more and no less than another form of business networking. You use it alongside your offline networking and marketing activity as a great way to motivate your target market and prospects to engage with you, buy from you and buy from you again.

The really savvy and switched on business winners have now realized that you need online and offline networking, ie joined-up networking tools and skills in your selling kit bag if you are going to get ahead of your competitors.

Heather Townsend, FT Guide to Business Networking

What is networking?

Networking is about interacting with people. Using networking effectively as part of your M2M marketing activity involves building and maintaining mutually beneficial relationships with your target market, named prospects and specific contacts. When you network effectively you have a purpose which is more than just meeting new people, cosy chats or working a room. Principled Sellers use business networking to:

● increase their profile;
● extend and strengthen the community around them;
● generate opportunities to win more business;
● build business insight and intelligence;
● learn new skills.

Principled Selling Tip: When you focus on relationships as their own reward lots of serendipitous things just happen.

Amazing things can happen when you develop relationships through business networking. While your networking activity needs to be planned and structured, unplanned and valuable opportunities present themselves. Getting this book published for instance started with a Tweet that within a few months led to a book proposal and formal offers from two leading publishers – one of which I had never actually met face to face.

While social networking is now being adopted as a credible alternative to face-to-face networking, the more traditional forms of networking still have their place. You just need to be strategic about where you network so that you are meeting as many of the right people as possible.

Winning business through networking

For information they trust, people go to:

● people similar to themselves;
● their social networks (online and offline);
● micro-blogging sites;
● websites which share valuable content.

Source: Edelman Barometer of Trust

When you use business networking effectively you tick all the boxes. You will be trusted as being a player in your target market, as someone who understands the clients' world and who invests in their world by sharing meaningful content through networking activities.

My colleague Heather Townsend in the *FT Guide to Business Networking,* identified that business relationships can be categorized on five levels.

FIGURE 6.1   Business relationships

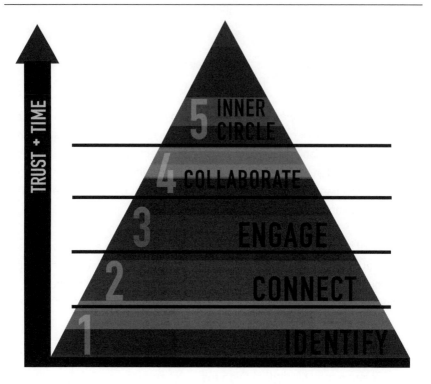

When used as part of your M2M marketing, the levels work like this:

Level 1: Identify

This is where someone first appears on your radar. They will be someone connected with your target market(s), who is associated with a named prospect or someone who is a specific contact, they could be on your list of dream customers. It is possible they found you before you found them because of your online networking activity. At this stage you know their name, but you have never communicated with them.

Level 2: Connect

You are communicating valuable content via social media that will attract the people you want to build a business relationship with. Connections are made on LinkedIn and maybe Facebook. You follow each other on Twitter or interact in a forum or other online discussion group. You are now having a one-way or two-way conversation via social media. Both parties are asking themselves if there is a benefit in getting to know each other better and if they like each other. Your valuable content is being shared 'virally' by those people who trust your content and find it useful and interesting.

Level 3: Engage

Before you can generate any business from a relationship or via a relationship, you need to get to at least this level. At Level 3 you continue to build trust via a phone call, video call (Skype) and a face-to-face meeting.

Level 4: Collaborate

Your relationship has now progressed sufficiently that you are both regularly communicating together. The relationship might have developed because the person has become a client and you use social media as one form of maintaining communication. It might have been that there was no immediate opportunity and you are staying on the radar of a future dream client. You will also be maintaining relationships where you will be helping each other in little or big ways, for example by sharing useful intelligence, passing business opportunities to each other or introducing each other to members of your network.

Level 5: Inner circle

There are plenty of Level 5 relationships around – people who like each other as well as doing business with each other. Sometimes the business relationship becomes so strong it turns into a personal friendship. Friendship doesn't automatically make a Level 5 relationship; Level 4 activities which make the relationship collaborative at a business level still need to exist.

When you understand which level a relationship is at, you can focus on investing in that relationship and business opportunities will follow.

How social media engages your prospects and clients

Social media as part your M2M marketing

The key in social media is to share things of value.

Charles H. Green, *Trusted Advisor*

Human beings like to connect with like-minded people; it is in the DNA of people to build communities. There is plenty of research by eminent psychologists that shows this is why social networking has had such a huge impact in such a short time. It is why recommendations from connections via social media are trusted more than advertising or old-style marketing.

FIGURE 6.2   How social media supports your M2M marketing

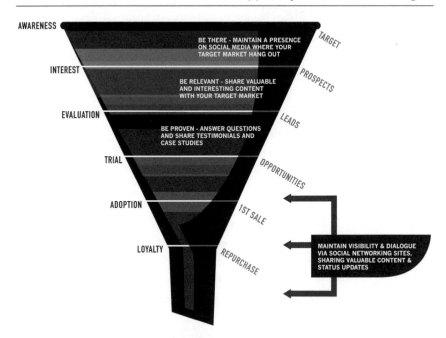

Reproduced with kind permission of Heather Townsend

Social media fits so well with M2M marketing and Principled Selling because it is a type of 'pull' marketing. You attract people to you by the messages you communicate, the valuable content you share, the profile you build and the conversations you have. While the search functionality of sites such as Twitter and LinkedIn can provide you with a massive ready-made prospect list, this shouldn't be used in the same way you use a mailing list or subscriber data-base. Just as you shouldn't go up to someone in a networking event and start to pitch your services to them, so you shouldn't do this on social media. Any busi-ness won via social media is built upon a foundation of trust and credibility, which is often built up over months rather than on the basis of one e-mail only.

Principled Selling Tip: Don't use social media as just another way to broadcast your sales messages.

Getting started on social media

You can be up and running with social media in minutes. There is little or no upfront cost; your biggest investment will be time:

● Decide why you want to use social media and how this will support your M2M marketing efforts. Social media should be part of your marketing effort but not your only marketing effort. You might use it to support valuable content campaigns, to increase visitor numbers to your website or to gain subscribers for your monthly e-newsletter.

● Using the selection criteria you developed for target markets, named prospects and specific contacts, identify who you want to attract and engage with on social media.

● Identify which social media sites you will use to connect with your chosen audience and to share your valuable content.

● Identify what your target audience will find useful and interesting to read.

● Decide what you want your target audience to do as a result of interacting with you via social media. Do you want them to sign up for a mailing list, be motivated to meet you, download your e-book or buy your book at a bookstore?

● Decide who within you organization will be responsible for communicating with your target audience. There is a time implication and the more people you can involve the better.

● Identify key performance indicators, processes and systems to enable you to measure the impact of your social media activity. This could be you tagging people in your CRM system when you have engaged with them on social media. Or it could be using Google analytics to measure how much traffic you are getting from social media and what visitors do when they visit your website.

● Finally, train up your team on how to use social media tools and how to build business relationships online.

Social media tools and how to use them

The term social media refers to the platforms that like-minded people use to connect, share information and build relationships. Like everything, social media has its own jargon, but don't let that put you off – with just a little understanding you can be up and running in no time. The most common social media platforms you are likely to use are:

● blogs;
● Twitter;
● LinkedIn;
● Facebook;
● YouTube;
● Google+;
● Pinterest;
● Online forums.

If you are new to social media, the platforms of most interest to you will be blogs, Twitter and LinkedIn. While some business-to-business organizations have a Facebook presence, it is generally most useful in business-to-consumer marketing.

What is a blog?

The term blog is a short for weblog or web log. When you write a blog, maintain a blog or add an article to an existing blog it is called *blogging*. Individual articles on a blog are called *posts* or *entries*. A person who posts the entries is called a *blogger*.

It is a powerful marketing and communication tool which helps you and your organization to communicate with prospects, customers and clients. You will develop better relationships and greater trust with your target market, named prospects and specific contacts.

As with all the social media tools mentioned here, you don't need any complex technical skills to use a blog. You can post to your blog site using articles you have written in Word documents. It is an easy and quick way to present your own material and you don't need the permission of a commissioning editor to publish it!

Your blog helps people to see beyond marketing messages, giving you an opportunity to share valuable content and to demonstrate that there are real human beings behind the products and services you provide.

CASE STUDY

'I've been writing copy for about 20 years and only came across the concept of writing valuable content relatively recently. At first I wasn't keen on the whole idea as I felt it went against the grain of everything I believed about the craft of concise copywriting. Twelve months later with a successful blog, my feelings are totally reversed. It is a really smart way for a business or individual to build their reputation.

The blog gives my company a way to share my knowledge and experience in a manner that just doesn't work in sales copy. We've become a trusted go to expert in our field and it helps us build long-term relationships with people we would otherwise never have been able to reach through traditional media. The value of that to us is priceless.

I'm a total convert. Writing content that has value for people is something I find immensely satisfying not least because it is attracting a string of new clients who now appreciate just how I can help them.'

Jim O'Connor, Stories That Sell LLC

Tweeting with Twitter

Twitter is what is known as a micro-blogging site. Users are called Tweeters who post short messages of up to 140 characters. Users choose people to follow and if you follow another user you see all their updates or Tweets. You can send an open message, reply to others' Tweets and if you and another user follow each other you can send a private direct message.

As a businessperson, Twitter is likely to be your number one social media platform for networking and engaging with potential clients. At present it's by far the most popular way of sharing a business-related blog article. It can work as well for salespeople, accountants, business owners and lawyers as it does for plumbers. It is easy to build up a targeted list of people that you'd like to connect with. With a limit of 140 characters, there's no room for waffle!

One of the great things about Twitter as part of your M2M marketing activity is that it allows everyone to contact everyone else. Past relationships or status doesn't matter and it allows you to start a discussion with all sorts of people in your target market and named prospects. It can also help you to connect with specific contacts. It's possible to build really powerful connections on Twitter, which are a fantastic way of attracting people to your content and expanding your network.

Principled Selling Tip: Don't fall into the trap as some do and just use Twitter to send out sales messages. You will soon find you lose your audience if you use it as just another database to broadcast to.

Frequency and content

Try to post at least three times a day. It's only 140 characters and doesn't take long. If you do business across different time zones you can even schedule Tweets to be posted at the time your followers are most likely to see them.

Your following will increase and you will become a popular Tweeter if your posts are roughly:

● one-third valuable content from your own sources (blogs, articles);
● one-third shared valuable content from other sources (Retweets);
● one-third social chat and general comments.

Valuable content from your own sources might include tips and sometimes links to your blog posts or articles. Try to resist promoting products or services in Tweets; it's a sure way to lose followers.

Retweets make sharing valuable content easy. The people you follow will supply you with lots of content, most of which is interesting and some of which your own followers will find interesting. One click and all your followers receive that content.

That last third of your Tweeting input is about showing you are human. It simply isn't the real world to be talking business in every conversation offline and it's the same online. That one-third social chat might be anything from your frustration with public transport this morning to mentioning a concert or show you are going to later. Some Tweeters share their favourite quotes, some discuss sport. Steer clear of politics and don't start or participate in arguments. Even if you feel strongly that you are right, you will waste time and inevitably alienate someone.

Connecting with LinkedIn

Often described as Facebook for professionals, membership of LinkedIn is growing at a phenomenal rate. Two new members sign up every second of every day. What you share on LinkedIn is your professional persona rather than anything personal. It is a place to connect with potential customers and clients, to use as a contact base and to share valuable content.

When someone wants to check you out – a prospect, a supplier or even a headhunter – the first thing they usually do is Google your name. If you are a member of LinkedIn your name will appear in the top few results. Your profile on LinkedIn is your online resume and you do need to ensure that the impression it gives of your brand is the one you want to give. There is an old saying that you only get one chance to make a first impression and you should make sure that the first impression people get of you on LinkedIn is the one you want them to have.

Probably the most important feature is the status update, which allows you to share information with your connections. You can let your connections know about product launches, new projects, new client wins and your latest blog, and share content that they will find useful.

CASE STUDY

Examples

- JMC International Trade Group in Shenzhen, Guangdong gets 75 per cent of its business from LinkedIn. They found that the quality of information, people and tools available on LinkedIn surpasses all other social networking sites in terms of business.
- Jason Itzowitch was contacted by someone who had heard of him through BNI – Business Network International. This person said that one of his BNI members in Las Vegas was organizing a Social Media conference and he needed a speaker. He submitted Jason's name to the organizer and he was one of four potential candidates. After the

organizer reviewed his profile and saw his recommendations, Jason was hired without the organizers interviewing anyone else. Jason recently returned from a second trip to Las Vegas where he did a significant amount of additional business – all because of LinkedIn.

- An open source solutions developer successfully leveraged LinkedIn Groups to promote their seminars and events. They shared valuable content in the form of slides, videos, articles and case studies and took part in discussion groups. The result was a 30 per cent increase in the number of delegates from target markets attending their seminars, a significant increase in brand awareness and a 15 per cent hike in sales.

Being personal with Facebook

Facebook is a personal social network which is for some businesses and not for others. Facebook's millions of users update their status regularly with personal stuff. Where they're going, how they're feeling, what they did last night. They share things that make them laugh, rant about things that annoy them, laugh, talk, flirt, argue. All human life is there. In short it's a vibrant, noisy, lively place where people let their hair down. If your business fits well into this upbeat, social environment, then starting a Facebook page for your business could be an excellent idea.

Go viral with YouTube

According to Mashable.com, YouTube was created when one founder, Jawed Karim, unsuccessfully searched for footage of Janet Jackson's now famous 'wardrobe malfunction', and when he and his two friends Chad Hurley and Steven Chen realized they could not share videos through e-mail because of attachment limitations. The three realized the missing link for sharing and sending videos, and YouTube was born.

YouTube isn't just a video platform, it is a social network. Because of YouTube's easy to use format, messages are spread quickly and effectively across a variety of media including Facebook and Twitter, embedded in websites and via e-mail. You can easily add a YouTube video to your website or your Facebook account, and the end-user does not need any special viewer to see your content.

Stories abound of videos 'going viral', with millions of views being totted up in a few days. In fact there is a whole video industry dedicated to producing videos designed with that specific purpose. They are professionally produced and can be very expensive. You may be lucky and find your content is so valuable and so entertaining that it will go viral or you may have the budget for professionals to help. You can still reap benefits if you use the video feature on your smart phone and upload that.

CASE STUDY

Brentcom provides business support services to small companies. Their video campaign was rolled out showcasing about 20 video testimonials from Brentcom's customers talking about the benefits of using the company's services.

"The videos help people connect on a more emotional level with what we're doing", said Sharon Heart, Director of Public Relations, who also handles valuable content marketing efforts. *"It shows how our clients are improving their own businesses using our services. Prospects don't always want to read the written word; they want quick communication with a face on it."* As well as posting to YouTube, the videos were put onto their blog, where they get lots of play and they were used as part of an integrated valuable content campaign.

The campaign produced significant results. In the year before the initiative was implemented, marketing produced 50 trackable enquiries. A year later the campaign generated 975 leads; last year it generated 1,800.

The sales team also uses the videos as sales collateral when customers request references, or want to hear a customer bring to life what it is like to work with the company and its products. Twitter is used to link back to videos and they are embedded in e-newsletters sent out to customers and prospects who have signed up on their mailing list.

The new pretenders and upstarts

The five main platforms – blogs, Twitter, LinkedIn, Facebook and YouTube – are likely to provide you with all the support you need for your M2M marketing activity.

New platforms come and go and the most discussed right now are Google+ and Pinterest. Google+ is Google's third attempt to crack the social media marketplace. It is a mixture of Twitter and Facebook, with the ability to segment who receives what updates from you. To date Google+ has 90 million users signed up, but only a small proportion of these users are regularly using and engaging with Google+.

Pinterest users can upload, save, sort and manage images, known as pins, and other media content (ie videos) through collections known as pinboards. Pinboards are generally themed so that pins can easily be organized, categorized and discovered by other users.

TABLE 6.1   How to use social media

Platform	B2C or B2B	Best for...	Principled Selling tips
Blogging	B2B and B2C	Encouraging website visitors to return regularly Communicating valuable content Creating marketing collateral SEO	Blog regularly Keep your blog posts short, ideally under 500 words
Twitter	B2B B2C	Networking with your target and market Named prospects and specific contacts Increasing traffic to your blog and website	Balance your Tweets so you have a mixture between sharing articles, updates and conversations Tweet daily, and ideally a minimum of 3 times Influencing journalists Don't push your sales and marketing messages
LinkedIn	B2B	Building a relationship with corporate decision makers Networking with potential introducers	Focus your updates on business matters Update your status at least once a week Use LinkedIn groups to increase your network's reach Complete your profile
Facebook	B2C	Engaging with consumers Sharing visual content	Keep your updates light and encourage users to interact with your page Only post up to a maximum of 3 times in one day
YouTube	B2B and B2C	Creating valuable content Displaying video content which can be reproduced on Facebook, your website and blog	Use your YouTube videos as marketing collateral Have a different YouTube channel for each of your market segments

TABLE 6.1 *continued*

Platform	B2C or B2B	Best for...	Principled Selling tips
Google+	B2B	Great exposure for your content to Google search engines Easily segment your message to people you want to read it Use the hangouts feature to have live video chats with your network, clients and prospective clients	Organize your Google+ contacts into circles Add a Google+ business page Add a Google +1 button to your website
Pinterest	B2C	Driving website traffic Connecting with audiences who like visual content Connecting with advocates and influencers Sharing pictures and images	Create boards that help you tell your story to the audiences you want to tell it to Pair every important piece of content with an eye-catching image Encourage engagement and pinning activity by allowing others to post their pins to your profile

The Principled Selling approach to social media

Make the investment

Being authentic is at the heart of social media. Be authentic in your communication, show genuine interest in helping your audience and your investment will lead to winning more business.

Sharon Tanton, co-author of *Valuable Content Marketing,* summed it up well in this recent guest blog for PrincipledSelling.org.

There are many different social media options and there will be others to come, but if you want to get the best results across any social media network the same approach applies.

- **Take part:** Social media *is* important – join the conversation or you're missing a trick – be sociable, communicate on the platforms and be consistent – show up regularly.

- **Give value:** Be helpful, entertaining, educate your clients – not self-promoting, annoying or boring – don't talk about yourself – know your customers – become a valuable source of information for others.

- **Be generous:** Share content and information, and be generous to others – share other people's content even more than your own – if it is valuable to your kind of customers, then share it – even if it's a competitor. Make 10 Tweets about others for every one Tweet you make about yourself. Become known as someone who offers things up to others, and you will attract people to come to you.

- **Be interesting:** Mix it up – all sorts of different types of content. Have something to say.

- **Be human:** People want to do business with those they know, like and trust – get people to know a little more about you – not just the work you do, but the whole of you, or at least as much as you feel willing to openly share.

- **Be focused:** Talk around your business mission – not relentlessly, but let the golden thread shine through your message so it's clear to those that follow you what you stand for.

- **Be polite:** Say thanks to those that follow and share your stuff.

Social media

- Have a strategy for who you want to attract and which social media platforms you will use.

- Share valuable content.

- Make sure your team are able to present a consistent brand on social media.

- Write and communicate a social media policy which is flexible enough to allow you to use social media, but minimize any risks to your company.

- Set a time limit on the amount of activity you will do on social media.

- Tailor your messages to your audience and social media platform.

A guide to offline networking

Mixing with A-listers

When networking is mentioned many people think of a room full of strangers who you are supposed to pretend to be interested in, collect business cards from and who you are supposed to sell something to. Some people think that it's about working the room to start the sales process or flying the flag, letting people know you and your company exist.

Networking isn't about starting the sales process, pitching your product or uncomfortable chats with people you know you will never do business with. It is about developing strong relationships through which future business opportunities will arise. You do business not with your network but *through* your network and building the right network takes time.

Networking is about meeting people in order to:

- generate opportunities to find prospects and referrals;
- increase your brand visibility (company and personal);
- strengthen and extend your sphere of influence;
- discover new ideas, tools and connections.

First of all you need to decide where you will network. There are established networking groups in almost every country and you are probably already inundated with invitations to attend free networking sessions. Remember that many networking groups are businesses in their own right and they depend on memberships fees. Be highly selective and only attend the events that your customers and potential clients are likely to attend or where attendees will be connected to your target audience. For instance, if you provide a service to small businesses, attend the events that small business owners attend but also the events that other non-competitive suppliers, such as business advisors and accountants might organize for them. People like to know there are others out there that they can refer their customers to.

Principled Selling Tip: Network where your target market, named prospects, customers and clients network.

Networking opportunities arise at exhibitions, conferences, professional asso-ciation events, seminars, hospitality events, fund raising events and at training courses. Actively seek opportunities to meet those people who will help you build your business. If you are invited to internal events in your own organization attend them too. If your company puts on events for clients, make sure you are invited. If you are not visible to the world you want to influence, you are invisible to those contacts that can help you grow your business.

At every event you attend there will be what Heather Townsend refers to as A-, B- and C-listers:

- A-listers: Those contacts well connected to your target market and who are likely to help you immediately achieve your business goals. They might become a referral source, introducer or new client.
- B-listers: Those contacts you enjoy meeting but who are unlikely to immediately help you achieve your business goals.
- C-listers: Contacts you meet but who are very unlikely to help you achieve your business goals.

It is worthwhile capturing the details of everyone you meet in your contact management system even if you don't intend to keep in touch, as you never know who people know!

CASE STUDY

I was on a Travel Book author's A-list, and I spotted something by one of my C-list contacts, about a TV producer on that person's C-list. Effectively, the producer was on the author's G-list and totally invisible. However, through the power of networking, within two hours the author had been invited by the producer onto a National TV breakfast show with her book *Two Feet Forward*. Filming has happened on the shore of Sydney Harbour, and it should air very soon.

Robert Watson, Business and writers coach

Please, please follow up!

You can't stay in your corner of the forest waiting for others to come to you. You have to go to them sometimes.

A.A. Milne, *Winnie the Pooh*

The single biggest mistake that people make about networking is failing to follow up. The follow up might be an agreed telephone contact to arrange a coffee. It might be that you plug the contact into your proactive valuable content campaign. Following up connections you make through your networking is easy, and just in case you worry about making that 'dreaded phone call', you will find out just how easy it is in the next chapter.

Summary

Business networking has never been easier using online and offline tools to help you win more business. Social media is a serious aid to your M2M marketing activities. The great news is you can get started in minutes and become famous in your target markets within weeks. Networking online in a highly targeted way gets you in front of the people you want to engage with and connects you with other influential individuals who will help you. Have as your goal building trusted relationships, sharing meaningful content and helping your audience, and you will find that social media is serendipitous. Avoid self-promotion and pitching your products and services and using the medium as just another database to broadcast your sales and marketing messages. Business will flow if you make the right investment. Be strategic about your offline networking and be highly targeted about where you network and who you want to meet.

Action points

- If you don't already have one, start a blog. Encourage colleagues to make contributions and aim to post one article each month.

- Sign up for a Twitter account and start following people in your target markets and named prospects.

- Many of the people you follow will follow you back on Twitter – you are now connected so say *Hi!*

- Tweet links to your blog and website.

- Make sure you appear on LinkedIn and that your profile gives a great first impression.

- Update your LinkedIn status with something of value at least once a week.

- Choose one offline networking event to attend in the next two months.

- Download the M2M social media scheduler from **www.principledgroup.com/resources**.

CHAPTER 7

M2B (MOTIVATING CUSTOMERS TO BUY)

Trust opens up new and unimagined possibilities.

Robert C. Solomon

Your M2M activity has one purpose – to build relationships with senior executives in order to meet them face to face. In this chapter we look at how to make follow-up calls to make an appointment to meet, how to prepare for meetings with senior executives, how to guide the meeting with a light touch and how to keep your prospect motivated to buy using the M2B (motivate to buy) approach.

Topics covered in this chapter

- How to get meetings with potential dream clients
- Preparing and structuring the perfect M2B meeting
- Using the Principled Selling E^3 model to make a powerful start

With the success that social media brings to building networks you could be forgiven for thinking that there isn't much need for face-to-face meetings any more. However, when your objective is to win long-term business with dream clients there is nothing better than meeting in person when it comes to building trust. Researchers at Cornell University found in-person meetings are better than virtual events at capturing people's attention, creating positive emotions and building long-term trusted relationships. The energy and personal connections that are made when there is human interaction can never be replicated using social media or even the phone. Relationships forged in person are always stronger.

How to get meetings with potential dream clients

Imagine the scene.

You are at the boardroom table of a business that could become a dream client. You have been welcomed by the CEO or other senior decision makers with the words *'I've been looking forward to meeting you'*. Jackets are off, the coffee and biscuits are out and a really comfortable business meeting is underway between two people motivated to be there. Imagine impressing your client with how you add value in the meeting, how you build trust and how you conduct the meeting. Imagine the meeting is going so well that they are motivated to do business with you and commit to the next step.

That is how selling can be. That is how selling must be if you are to stand the best chance of winning a client who will contribute to helping you grow your business and achieve your vision.

How different is that meeting to the many 'selling' meetings you have probably done which are anything but comfortable – where sometimes the seller doesn't really want to be there and the potential buyer is clock-watching.

The first meeting you have with a potential dream client is *really* important. Getting face to face is where you will be able to build on the relationship already established through your valuable content and social media activities. It is where you will be able to demonstrate your congruent approach to business and Principled Selling and where you will stand out from competitors.

The meeting is typically one hour long – 60 minutes where you will have the opportunity to further motivate your prospect to want to buy from you. Sixty minutes that will move you closer to winning business from a customer who could become a dream client who will buy and re-buy from you.

This hour is a real 'golden hour'.

How to follow up a lead

The great news is that when you get really good at providing valuable content and networking activities some client's will be motivated enough to contact you and ask to meet you. Phew – no need for that dreaded phone call to follow up!

*Principled Selling Tip: Y*ou have to follow up leads if you want to win more business.

That dreaded phone call

No matter how good your valuable content activities and social media have been there will always be a need to be proactive and make outbound phone calls to connect with your dream client.

You may need to make the call to:

● follow up on a valuable content campaign;

● follow up on an offline networking event;

● follow up on contact made online;

● follow up a referral.

Intellectually the people I have worked with 'get' that a phone call is necessary. They know waiting for the phone to ring is a strategy for business failure. But ...

They don't make the calls.

Why not? Because before understanding the Principled Selling approach they felt that they had to call strangers. These 'strangers' might reject them or might react negatively to having their day interrupted by someone trying to push something they are not interested in. But that's not how it will be if you follow the Principled Selling approach. You won't be calling strangers; you will be contacting people who are expecting your call and are motivated to speak with you.

The other reason people don't like to make the phone call is that they have never been trained in how to do it. Full-time salespeople do get in-depth training but it sometimes teaches all sorts of manipulative techniques that you will never need.

Forget having a list of objection-handling techniques; forget trying to get around 'gatekeepers' such as PAs. You won't need those techniques if you follow the Principled Selling approach.

Preparing to make a follow-up call

The key rule about making follow-up phone calls is that you have only one objective: **to make an appointment for a meeting.**

This is a really important rule. Long-term profitable relationships are not built over the phone and therefore it is vital not to attempt to pitch or get involved in deep discussions about your product or service.

There are five simple steps to making an appointment over the phone:

1 the greeting;

2 make a link;

3 ask for an appointment;

4 deal with questions;

5 confirm the appointment.

Before actually calling to make an appointment here are a few tips:

Make the call when you are feeling upbeat

A telephone amplifies moods. If you are feeling less than positive on Monday it's best to put the call off until the following day when you will feel more upbeat. If you find that you arrive at Thursday and still don't feel upbeat, then on Friday you have to make the call anyway – you promised to call this week and delivery on even the smallest promises matters.

Write it down – but don't use a script

On stage, TV or movies actors are believable because they sound natural. They have learned their lines from a script but they don't use a script to deliver the words. It's the same when using the phone to make an appointment. Nothing sounds worse on the telephone than someone reading from a script.

It will help however to write down the words you are going to use and then practise until you get the words right without reading them. This isn't an oner-ous task – there won't be many words to remember. The art of making the phone call is remaining conversational at all times, you don't need to suddenly go into a pitching mode. Just imagine you are calling a valued client who you already know... and relax. Senior executives tend to have busy diaries, so be prepared to suggest a meeting three or even four weeks away.

Imagine for a moment that you are Jon Saunders of Mercer Software and you are following up after a proactive valuable content campaign to Karen Walker, a senior executive with a target prospect. You wrote three letters and enclosed information with each letter that was appropriate and interesting for the prospect. In the final letter you mentioned that you would be calling to fix an appointment to meet.

Many people, even senior decision makers, have direct lines these days, so for now we will assume Karen answers the phone.

A typical call might go something like this:

Greeting

Karen: *Karen Walker.*

Jon: *Hi Karen, this is Jon Saunders of Mercer Solutions.*

Karen: *Hi Jon.*

Make a link

Jon: *Karen, you might recall that I've sent you a few pieces of information recently. I hope you have found them interesting?*

Karen: *Yes I did thanks Jon, really relevant to some of the projects I'mworking on right now.*

Jon: *Great, I'm pleased. I'm calling as promised to fix a date to meet.*

Karen: *Yes, you mentioned you'd call in your last letter. That article on cloud-based applications really got me thinking. Is that something you specialize in?*

(There is a risk here that Jon gets embroiled in a conversation over the phone that really ought to wait until he is face to face. We need to acknowledge the interest and remember that our objective is to fix an appointment to meet.)

Jon: *There's a lot of interest in cloud-based applications right now and it is one of the solutions we have available. I'll be more than happy to chat about it when we meet. How about Tuesday 17th at 10.30?*

Karen: *Yes that looks fine.*

Jon: *Tuesday 17th at 10.30; I look forward to it.*

It really can be that easy if you have built a trusted reputation for you and your business before telling your own story.

Dealing with resistance

A number of the prospects you want to meet will have their calls directed through a personal assistant. Some salespeople will use dubious techniques to get around the PA, who they often see as a gatekeeper intent on stopping any salespeople speaking with their boss. Principled Sellers don't resort to tricks and they acknowledge that the PA has a job to do. Part of that job is to filter out people who might be an unwelcome interruption to their own and their boss's day. Here again is one of the advantages of using a valuable content campaign. A good PA will know what their boss received from you and will be expecting your call, just as the prospect will, and will put your call straight through.

When you call you might be asked what your call is about. If you are, simply respond: *'I've recently been in touch with Karen and she's expecting my call to arrange a meeting.'* This will work for almost all calls that go through a PA – if you have built a trusted reputation before trying to sell! Anything else is a cold-call and Principled Sellers never cold-call. Resist any temptation to explain any more than you are calling to make an appointment and just as importantly be courteous and professional towards the PA. You definitely want them on your side.

As I've said before, winning business is not an exact science. We can maximize the opportunities by getting things right, but even when we do get them right, things may not go quite so smoothly. You may experience some resistance from the prospect you want to meet with.

It may be that the prospect says something like *'What you sent was very interesting but we don't have any budget right now'.* The time to explore budgets is when you meet; at this stage neither party knows what costs might be involved if you do business together. You can therefore respond, *'I understand and at this stage I have no idea if there will be any opportunity to work together. I'm really keen to meet with you to explore if there is anything we do that might help you now or in the future'* – then ask for the appointment as before.

You might be told that the prospect already has a provider of the service or product you supply. Your response to that might be *'Most of our existing customers had a supplier when we first met them. I have no idea at this stage if there will be an opportunity to do business together and I'm really keen to explore if there is anything we might help you with now or in the future'* and again ask for the appointment.

But what if the resistance continues? In my first sales job working for an international brand I was given a list of about twenty answers to common reasons prospects would give to avoid making an appointment. It felt crass then and it certainly is today. If the prospect is giving one reason after another not to meet they are telling you that they are not motivated to spend time with you – for now. There is no point wearing the prospect down so that they give in to making an appointment. The appointment will be cancelled or worse you will turn up and the prospect will resent being manipulated – not a great start to a first meeting with a prospect that could have become a dream customer.

Much better to pick up the signals long before any frustration with you sets in. If the prospect gives more than one or two reasons that it's not a good use of their time to meet, then say *'I understand that a meeting would not be a productive use of your time right now. Are you happy for me to keep in touch with anything that might be of interest?'* To which the response is almost always Yes. Then say *'I'll make a note to call again in, say, three months. Is that OK?'*

If you have been congruent in your approach to business development the prospects you call will not be cold-calls. Most will accept your call and most will agree to meet with you when the time is right for them.

Preparing and structuring the perfect M2B meeting

Preparing to meet a potential dream customer

CASE STUDY

'I arrived fully prepared to give a 40 minute presentation and the buyer pulled out an egg timer! This buyer certainly wasn't motivated to meet me. I realized that my entire marketing and sales approach needed to be redesigned.'

Kate Sandler, Account Manager, snack food manufacturer

Differentiating through business development involves being better than your competitors at the small things. Even your biggest and most experienced competitors get lax about their preparation for business development meetings with prospective customers and clients.

Confirming the appointment in writing is one of those small things you can do that a competitor might not do. Add something of value to that confirmation and you will definitely stand out from the crowd. If the meeting is several weeks ahead consider maintaining enthusiasm by sending more valuable content.

Principled Selling Tip: When you write to confirm an appointment attach some valuable content.

Another element of preparation is making sure you turn up on time for the meeting. Turning up on time is about more than being courteous. It's about demonstrating that you deliver on your promises. You don't want to start a first meeting with someone who could become an ideal client by making excuses for being late. Very early in my career my first sales manager, Dave Philips, said to me 'David, people don't arrive late; they set out late', and that is so true.

Potential customers have heard all the excuses for being late you could ever think of. Be different by always being punctual.

On that rare occasion when you do arrive late never ever blame anyone else other than yourself. Take responsibility, demonstrate vulnerability and say something like 'I'm sorry I was late, I misjudged how long it would take to get here on time'. You will be amazed at the positive effect this will have on a new business relationship.

Reception routine

You will have worked hard to build a reputation with your potential customer and they are looking forward to meeting you. How you behave at every stage of the business development process will be noted and particularly so when you arrive at your prospect's office. Remember you are on show from the moment you arrive within the sight of your potential customer – and any of their staff. This is not the time to let down your guard, so assume the CEO has spotted you even as you park your car. If you think that is being too detailed then think again.

CASE STUDY

'In a previous job I'd arranged for the CEO of an important target prospect to meet my boss and me. I'd been working to get this particular appointment for months and I was excited about getting the opportunity to be meeting with the CEO – I'd had a great telephone conversation with her and she was really keen to meet. I'd arranged to meet my boss for a coffee close by the prospect's offices 45 minutes before the meeting but he called to say he was running late, which to be honest was not that unusual for him.

'When I arrived at the prospect's offices there were no visitors' car parking spaces available so I had to park about a ten minute walk away. I called my boss and said I'd meet him in reception and I was there ten minutes early. With two minutes to go my boss turned up looking a bit hurried but he soon put on his 'professional' persona and we waited to be invited to the meeting room. We were ushered into the boardroom and a few moments later the CEO arrived. Before we had time to even smile and introduce ourselves she said 'Do you have a reason for parking in a disabled parking space?' My boss responded 'Ah, that would be me, the traffic was particularly busy, I was right on the last minute and there were no visitor parking bays available.' My heart sank when the CEO said 'Well please move it now, my PA who has a real need for a disabled space is waiting to park.' I was so embarrassed, at that moment if a hole had appeared I would have crawled into it.

'The meeting eventually started twenty minutes late. We never recovered the situation and we never did business with that CEO. My boss blamed the prospect rather than himself. I left there a few months later.'

Steve L, Key Account Manager, office equipment supplier

Principled Selling Tip: Have a reputation for punctuality; plan to arrive 15 minutes before every meeting, internal or external.

Getting this apparently small stuff right matters – a lot. When it comes to deciding who to buy from in an increasingly competitive marketplace, you should make sure you are the one who gets the small stuff right. Maybe your competitor won't and then you have a differentiator just by how you develop business.

OK, so you have got the time sorted. You have arrived at the prospect's reception around 10 minutes early (any earlier might put pressure on the person you are there to meet).

As you arrive at reception, looking and feeling relaxed and professional, you have the opportunity to make a positive impression on anyone you meet. Treat all the people you meet as if they were the CEO and that includes the receptionist. Increasingly senior executives will ask their front-line people what they think of potential suppliers. They know that some visitors put on their best behaviour for the CEO but behave less well towards those they perceive as having no influence. They want to know if what they have experienced is the genuine you or just an act.

Front-line staff are also involved more and more in project teams which just might be asked to consider you as a supplier. You have everything to gain by treating all your prospect's employees as you would the CEO and nothing to lose.

You can help the receptionist to do their job by giving them your business card as you give them your name. I think I have a fairly simple last name, Tovey, but over the years have got used to speaking my name and then spelling it out T O V E Y to ensure its doesn't get written down as Tobey, Toby or Todey! Letting the receptionist have your business card takes away all doubt.

As you are a few minutes early you will often be asked to take a seat and if you would like a coffee or other drink while you wait.

I suggest a polite refusal on the coffee and never sit down in a reception area. Reception seating is usually designed for aesthetics, not comfort or ease of getting out of. Imagine the scene. You are seated in the semi-reclined position afforded by most reception seating, briefcase in one hand and a coffee cup in the other when the CEO appears to greet you hand outstretched. You struggle to get up with no free hand to help you and are unable to shake hands. How does this look from the CEO's perspective as they approach you? Ungainly, uncomfortable, unprofessional and clumsy are words that come to mind. It's not a great first impression.

That first impression is so important. If you remain standing in the reception area (while avoiding being an obstruction) you will look and feel alert, comfortable and professional. You can check out any company information available which may provide you with insight and topics that you can ask questions about. If there is no company information, there is usually a business newspaper to read. Now imagine how it looks to an approaching CEO. They see you standing in reception, looking professional, calm, showing interest and ready to do business – a much better first impression.

Often, if you are meeting a senior executive, their PA or secretary will be the person to collect you from reception. Again, their impression of you matters.

Using the Principled Selling E³ model to make a powerful start

The power of the three Es

A first meeting is a golden opportunity for you to continue to build a trusted relationship with a potential dream client. Structuring your first meeting using the three Es will give the best chance of winning business – but for now you have to forget that your ultimate aim is to exchange your product or service for money.

It might seem strange advice in a book about helping you win more business to suggest that it shouldn't be your objective to walk away with an order; nevertheless this is the most successful mindset to have if you want start a long-term profitable relationship. You will sell more and make more profit when you adopt this thinking.

Having as your prime objective walking out of the first meeting with an order creates a problem for you. It changes the dynamics and communication needed to build trust and motivation. The way you communicate verbally and through body language when you are there to make a sale risks giving out all the wrong signals. You risk spending the meeting always seeking opportunities to push your ideas, to have your say, pouncing on what looks like buying signals and trying to close the sale. That is the antithesis of Principled Selling and far less effective.

The objectives for the first meeting are to:

- motivate your prospect to engage with you in the meeting;
- fully understand the prospect's requirements;
- build trust by being genuinely interested;
- add value by providing meaningful information that will help your prospect;
- gain commitment to a way forward after the meeting.

When these are your objectives you and your prospect will be more relaxed, you build trust and your prospect will be more motivated. With the Principled Selling approach your intention is to find the best way forward for the customer – which might of course be to agree to do business with you on the day.

The E³ model

Figure 7.1 shows how an E³ meeting should ideally be structured:

FIGURE 7.1 How to structure an initiation meeting

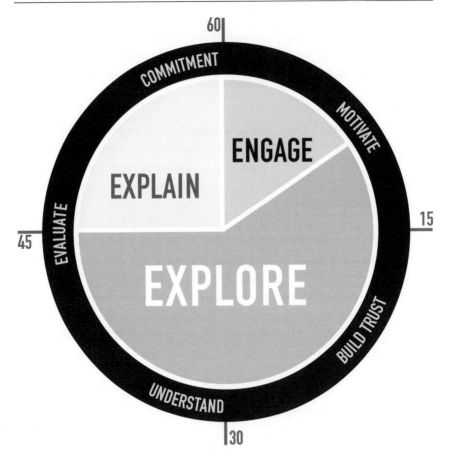

The three Es:

● **Engage** – motivate the prospect to answer your questions.
● **Explore** – use perceptive questioning and active listening to understand and build trust.

● **Explain** – provide meaningful advice and gain commitment to the way forward.

The E^3 model turns the traditional sales approach on its head. Often sellers use so much of the available time to pitch their wares and provide persuasive arguments that they miss the opportunity to really understand the prospect and build trust.

To be most effective, allocate your time in a first meeting like this:

- Engaging about 10 per cent of the meeting.
- Exploring about 60 per cent of the meeting.
- Explaining about 30 per cent of the meeting.

Engaging

This part of the meeting will only take five or six minutes. It is about getting the initial courtesies and formalities right and about positioning. It is not an opportunity to start pitching or download your experience and knowledge. There will be a time when it is your turn to enthusiastically present what you can do for the prospect, but that time is not now. You have not yet earned the right.

Having arrived in the meeting room there is the usual formality of a hand-shake. Handshakes are a sign of trust and help build strong relationships. First impressions do count and getting the business handshake right is something to master.

Principled Selling Tip: Handshakes mean different things in different cultures. Expect a firm handshake to mean confidence in most of Europe or the USA, whereas a limp handshake is the norm in Africa. A few seconds is about right in Europe and the USA, while in Africa the handshake may last a few minutes.

Another thing to get right is exchanging business cards. Here again there are cultural differences to be aware of. Best practice is to treat all business cards with respect; hold a card with both hands and read what is on the card. Reading a business card will sometimes provide you with new information.

Principled Selling Tip: If there are several people in the meeting on the prospect's side, laying their business cards out in front of you acts as an easy reminder of names and who is sitting where.

When it is time to start it is your responsibility to guide the meeting, but not in a heavy-handed controlling way. Guiding the meeting is much more about leadership, positive influence and maintaining motivation. It's about helping the prospect get the best out of the meeting and also ensures that the status of you and the prospect remains on equal terms.

So far you have worked hard to build a reputation and enough trust to motivate a senior decision maker to meet you. To suddenly change gear when face to face and present a sort of *gotcha* or *now it's my turn* approach risks undermining everything that earned you the right to get to this stage.

When the preliminaries are completed instigate your light-touch guidance by doing two things: check timing and position the meeting, your company and yourself.

As soon as business cards are exchanged and coffee, tea, etc. have been served, say something like *'We scheduled an hour for the meeting, is that still OK with you?'*

It is part of your job to be aware of timing throughout the meeting. It shows professionalism and courtesy towards your potential client that you respect their time.

Most of the time the response will be that the scheduled hour is confirmed and sometimes, because you did such a great job of earning the right to the meeting through your valuable content marketing, you will be told you have whatever time it takes.

Positioning your company, yourself and the meeting

During the early stage of the meeting it is important that your potential client engages with you. Good positioning will motivate them to take part and provide you with the vital insight that will help you to win business.

You can transition from checking the time available by saying something like:

'I'm not sure how much you know about me and my company; would it be helpful if I spent just a couple of minutes giving you a brief overview?'

The emphasis here is on *brief*. It is more than likely that the prospect has done some research on your company even if was just to Google you. They will have the basics and a feel for who you are. Now is not the right time to be giving chapter and verse about your company history and how great you are. At this stage you don't know whether what you see as a key benefit of dealing with you might be seen as the opposite by your prospect. You might say something that results in the perception that you are not right for their business.

You might have heard of the 'elevator pitch'. It is based on the idea that you should introduce your company in a way that is interesting and leaves the listener wanting more in two minutes – the time of the typical elevator ride.

I recently read a piece of research that confirmed my suspicion that most people don't recall what the seller says in a first meeting. The study suggested that a prospect will remember only one thing a week after your meeting. Sadly you don't get to choose what that one thing is. To counter this, salespeople learn their elevator pitch, a highly polished compelling story outlining their unique selling points and company history. On the receiving end it sounds like a sales 'spiel' – a form of words rolled out anytime someone stops long enough for the salesperson to rattle out their elevator pitch.

The people you want to do business with are busy; they, like you, live in a world full of information from dozens of sources competing for their attention. Often an elevator pitch doesn't have context, which is what a potential customer needs to make sense of what you say. Buyers are not usually experts in your field, so they need to hear something that makes sense in their world.

What you say about your company should be adapted to suit the market sector and the particular prospect you are meeting. If you have private and public sector clients, then you might have different positioning statements for each.

Your company statement

- Make it short.
- Adapt it to the audience.
- Make it relevant and cover who you help, the issues they have and the outcomes your solution achieves.

- Who you are.
- Finish with what clients get from working with you.

> A supplier of branded promotional goods who wants to win business from a financial services company might say:
>
> 'As you would expect, we provide the full range of high-quality branded promotional goods sourced from the best manufacturers. We specialize in working with high-profile brands for which sponsorship of major events remains an important part of their consumer marketing.
>
> Our clients in financial services tend to have to balance their need for promotional activity to maintain customer loyalty and attract new customers with the pressure on marketing budgets and a need to stay aligned with their corporate social responsibility policies. Providing promotional items that customers actually find useful and that they will continue to use has always been a challenge. Traditionally placing orders for large volumes of product was necessary to keep unit price low, which resulted in high levels of wastage.
>
> We are able to supply ethically sourced high-quality products that reflect our customers brand values while being able to provide quick turnaround on small volumes and still keep unit prices low. Our customers can stay within their budgets, reduce wastage and provide promotional items where the brand message will live on well after any events.
>
> I work on the national accounts team and spend all my time working with the financial services sector. My background is financial services marketing and I've seen how sales and consumer loyalty can be increased by providing branded promotional items that consumers want to own and will continue to use after an event.
>
> Some of my customers have been with us for ten years or more. They tell us that we are good at spending time to understand their business, that our people will go beyond the call of duty to help them and that we always deliver the quality they need within their budget.'

There is no need to pitch, no need for a long sales spiel, just some well-chosen words that will be enough to have your prospect thinking they would like to know more. Your words will not be the same as above, but if you keep to the same structure it will work for you.

Principled Selling Tip: Avoid long elevator pitches that talk about you – focus on the outcomes customers get from doing business with you.

Your positioning statement

Fill in the blanks below:

- Who my company helps: _____
- The issues they have are: _____
- The outcomes our solution achieves are: _____
- My role is: _____
- Customers say they like working with us because: _____

The next step is to position the meeting – getting agreement to your objectives and finding out what objectives your potential customer might have. A prospect who understands why you are asking probing questions will be more motivated to give you full answers.

Positioning the meeting

'I'm not sure whether there will be anything we can help you with right now but as you know we both thought it worthwhile meeting to explore what opportunities there might be. My objective over the next hour is to understand more about your organization and I'd like to ask you some questions and then share with you anything about our products and services that might be of useful to you. Is there anything you would like to cover?'

Having engaged your potential client, you are ready to move to the next step in the E^3 model – Explore. Explore is covered in the next chapter where you will learn about the skills and behaviours that will build trust and motivate your prospect to give you a full understanding of their requirements.

Summary

You have motivated your potential dream clients to meet you; they have been impressed by the valuable content you share. You need never worry about making a cold-call ever again; all you have to do is phone to make an appointment and arrange to meet with someone who is keen to speak with you. Make sure you don't get involved in detail on the call, don't use tricks to get around any resistance and remember that the sole purpose is to arrange an appointment.

Getting the small stuff right is really important. Your aim is to differentiate yourself and your organization by *how* you win business. A potential dream client is looking forward to meeting you and you have an opportunity to continue to impress them by how you prepare and how you conduct yourself. Guide the meeting with a light touch and use the Principled Selling E^3 model to structure the meeting. Engage your prospect with a well-developed and relevant positioning statement and motive them to answer your questions.

Action points

- Prepare your script for making follow-up calls.
- Practice until you don't need to read from the script.
- Prepare your responses to potential resistance.
- For every meeting carry with you a reminder of the E^3 model.
- Make a reminder note on your pad for each meeting that your objective is to build a trusted relationship.
- Prepare an outline positioning statement that introduces you and your company and that positions the meeting. Remember to adapt what you say for different audiences.
- Practise opening a meeting using the E^3 structure with your colleagues until you are comfortable with how to fully engage a potential dream client and motivate them to answer your questions.
- Use the templates and reminder in the Principled Selling Growth Model available to download at **www.principledgroup.com/resources**

CHAPTER 8

M2B (MOTIVATE TO BUY) SKILLS AND BEHAVIOURS

The wisest mind has something yet to learn.

George Santayana

Chapter 7 introduced you to making an appointment, preparing to meet a potential dream client and how to structure a first meeting using the Principled Selling E³ model. You have given your elevator pitch, have started to exercise light-touch guidance and have motivated your potential dream client to answer your questions.

Following the E³ model, you have Engaged. It is now time to *Explore*.

Topics covered in this chapter

- Building trust through understanding
- Advanced communication skills for Principled Sellers
- If you want to win business – shut up!
- Explore to guarantee understanding

Building trust through understanding

Seek first to understand

Seek first to understand, then to be understood.

Dr Stephen Covey, *The Seven Habits of Highly Effective People*

When I ask groups I work with what the most common reason is for them or their colleagues losing a sale, the answer is almost always 'price'. When I follow up by asking how they won their best customers, I never get one-word answers. When people explain how they won their best clients, their faces and voices tend to brighten up and they become animated as they enthusiastically share their stories about winning a great client:

- 'We invested time getting to know them.'
- 'We really understood their requirements.'
- 'We got deep insight into their business and critical success factors.'
- 'There was a good fit – the right chemistry between us.'
- 'Our proposal was right on the button.'
- 'Our presentation was like poetry in motion.'
- 'There was a negotiation about price as you'd expect – we were both happy with what was agreed.'
- 'It was hard work but fun.'

When a sale to a potential long-term client is lost it is rarely due to price alone. The main reason that relationships don't blossom is that not enough time and effort is invested in fully understanding customer's requirements. If you don't fully understand their requirements, then you can't put forward the right proposal, you don't build trust, you can't make the best presentation and it is unlikely to be much fun.

The iceberg principle

The iceberg principle is a term used to describe the writing style of Ernest Hemingway, the American writer. He learned to write in a surface level way where he omitted or hinted at the real point of a story. Hemingway believed that the true meaning of a piece of writing should not be evident at the surface level because the crux of a story lies below the surface. Sometimes known as the theory of omission, it provided him with a very distinctive but often frustrating style of writing.

When people begin a new relationship they tend to share information that is in the same style as Hemingway – they give their surface level story, only sharing the full picture with those close to them or people they trust. You don't have to be a ship's captain to know that an iceberg is only around 10 per cent above the water, with 90 per cent lying under the surface. For a ship it is the 90 per cent that the Captain doesn't see that is the dangerous part. The iceberg principle also applies to business relationships. Most prospects have their stories of 'omission' – the information about themselves and their business that they share with people they only have surface level relationships with. It isn't an attempt to deceive or catch you out; it is just what normal people do.

The risk is that a relationship is often sunk before it can flourish, not because of lack of understanding about the surface story, the prospect's story of omission, but a lack of understanding about the full picture.

FIGURE 8.1   Iceberg principle

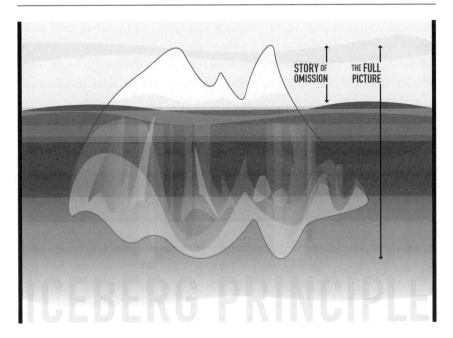

To win a dream client you have to be the one who they allow to get beyond their story of omission and who gains the insight that comes from getting below their iceberg.

Emotion drives decision making

The most successful salespeople know that emotions drive buying decisions. However much organizations attempt to make it appear that they only make rational decisions, human beings just can't avoid it.

The reasons are down to physiology. Studies into the emotional brain by Dr Joseph LeDoux, a neuroscientist at New York University, revealed that emotions drive decision making because the neural pathways running from the emotional area of the brain (the amygdala) to the thinking areas are wider and faster than those that run from the thinking areas back to the emotional area. Emotional impulses travel faster and with a greater 'bandwidth' than logic. If you are unsure, just think about how most people buy cars, books from a bookstore, holidays, houses or clothes. Think about how many CEOs put extensive research documents to one side and ask fellow board members how they 'feel' about a major decision.

Needs and wants

When considering a purchase all potential buyers have a set of requirements made up of needs and wants. Needs are easy to identify. They tend to be logical, rational and technical and they form part of a buyer's story of omission, the surface level story that they share with everyone. Wants are much more difficult to identify, for the seller and the buyer. Wants tend to be driven by emotion and because emotion is involved Wants are more difficult to communicate. Your potential customers will only share the full picture about their requirements when they trust you. Sharing with you that they feel vulnerable or how important a decision is to the success of their business or information about their personal ambition is often just as difficult for them to express as it is for you to discover.

Before you can put forward an effective solution in a way that will convince someone that they should buy from your company, you have to understand their needs *and* wants.

Principled Selling Tip: Wants can include the desire to reduce personal risk when making a decision, the desire to look good in front of a boss or a personal bias.

TABLE 8.1   Requirements = needs + wants

Needs	Wants
Logical	Emotional
Rational	Feelings
Technical	Values
Facts	Experience
Easy to communicate	Difficult to communicate

Advanced communication skills for Principled Sellers

Be unconsciously competent

The great news is that most people don't need to adopt new skills to win more business; they simply need to adapt skills they use very effectively in other parts of their lives. The most important communication skills you need to perfect at the Explore stage of a first meeting are questioning, listening and non-verbal communication. They are all skills that most people use instinctively every day.

While everyone tasked with winning more business may have the ability to ask questions and listen, the most successful are *unconsciously competent*. When you reach the level of unconscious competence in questioning and listening you are operating in the zone of advanced communication skills.

If you have ever learned to drive a car you will be familiar with moving from unconscious incompetence to unconscious competence.

Unconscious competence = 'Oh, anyone can drive a car, it looks easy'

Conscience incompetence = 'Oh no, I keep stalling the engine'

Conscious competence = 'Look, I am changing gear all the time without grinding them!'

Unconscious competence = 'OMG, I don't even know how I swerved to avoid that dog and didn't skid off the road'

FIGURE 8.2   Conscious competence

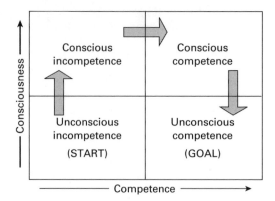

The art of powerful questions

I have no special talents; I am only passionately curious.

Albert Einstein

Most of what humans know about their world today came about because people were curious. People who have left a lasting legacy, like Einstein or Steve Jobs for instance have done, did so because they were genuinely curious and searched for the right questions to ask. *Stay Hungry, Stay Foolish* was Steve Jobs exhortation and encouragement to a graduating class of Stanford University. If you haven't seen it, look up the video on YouTube; it is really inspiring. He was imploring the graduation class not to be too easily satisfied or to get too complacent and to have an insatiable desire to learn. The curiosity that needs to be nurtured, he said to the students, is the search for knowledge.

Powerful questions are based on a genuine curiosity about your potential dream customer's world. How you can help a prospect becomes self-evident to you and to them when you ask the right questions and demonstrate genuine interest.

Principled Selling Tip: Ask questions to understand, not to demonstrate your knowledge.

It becomes more difficult to ask the right questions if you are searching for the answer you want. Some people even believe they should never ask a question they don't already know the answer to. The problem is that when you ask a question to get the answer you want or when you ask questions that you already know the answer to, today's more sophisticated buyers perceive it as manipulative and choose how they answer very carefully.

Watch any formal public hearing or commission to see how those under scrutiny carefully consider the consequences of how they answer a question. You can see in their faces they are weighing up what was really meant by the question and asking themselves if it is leading to a place that they don't want to go to.

The agenda trap

There are occasions when an agenda is not appropriate, and your first meeting with a potential dream client is a good example. At this stage an agenda stifles conversation and restricts your opportunity to get beyond the story of omission.

Don't try to find the 'pain'

I watched an interview on YouTube where a training consultant from a global sales training provider was very enthusiastically claiming that customers always lie and that it's the salesperson's job to quickly find out their real business pain and to uncover what keeps a prospect awake at night.

If that approach and mindset ever worked, it certainly isn't appropriate in today's business environment. I understand what sales trainers are trying to do. They want salespeople to sell benefits not features, to sell solutions to problems not just go on about their product or service. They don't want to waste time and want to get straight to the pain points that they think they can provide solutions to.

There are two problems with the finding the pain approach. It sounds like manipulation and can feel like a lack of consistency. There is a significant risk that what a prospect hears isn't *'What keeps you awake at night'* but *'How can I sell you something as quickly as possible'*.

It is important that the messages in your marketing communications match you the words you and you colleagues say during face-to-face meetings. The dynamics of a meeting can change in an instant if a potential buyer feels manipulated. They become selective about the information they provide and fail to give you the insight that would help you to deliver the best solution.

The sales 'pounce'

The mistake of creating questions to find pain points to provide the answer you want or to get to the sale as quickly as possible is that you are playing in the story of omission or the needs territory, and the sales 'pounce' is an inevitable consequence. At the first sight of a pain point the questions stop and the premature presentations start.

Constructing the right questions

Constructing the right questions lies at the heart of effective communications and information exchange. By using the right questions in a particular situation, you can improve a whole range of communications skills; for example, you gather better information and learn more; you build stronger relationships, and you help others to learn too. The questions you ask should be constructed in the context of the products and services you provide.

There are five types of questions Principled Sellers use to explore the prospect's world:

● open questions;
● open specific questions;
● reflective questions;
● summarizing questions;
● closed questions.

Open questions

I keep six honest serving-men, they taught me all I knew; their names are What and Why and When and How and Where and Who.

Rudyard Kipling

Open questions tend to elicit longer answers. They usually begin with what, why, how. An open question asks a prospect for their knowledge, opinion or feelings. *Tell me...*, *Explain...* and *Describe...* can also be used for developing an open conversation and finding out what is uppermost in the mind of the prospect.

Examples of open questions:

- *Tell me about your business.*
- *What are your critical success factors?*
- *How will the restructuring affect you?*

The most important feature of an open question is that it allows the other person to answer based on their own agenda. You demonstrate your genuine interest by letting the other person choose what they talk about in the context of the E^3 meeting; and their response is usually what is uppermost in their mind.

Open specific questions

Open specific questions are used to explore a particular topic, to gain deeper insight. *'Tell me about your holiday'* is an open question that allows the other person to choose where they begin their answer. *'Tell me about the hotel facilities'* is still an open question but influences the scope of the answer in order to get insight into a specific topic. Asking open specific questions is really useful to help you to guide an E^3 meeting with a light touch.

Reflective questions

You use these to reflect on tone or feelings.

- *I **think** what you are saying is...?*
- *That **sounds** like you would be forced into a difficult position with the support crew.*
- *So if you take the first option you would be **frustrated** because that undoes all the hard work of the last year.*

Summarizing questions

Summarizing questions are used to clarify and confirm what has been said:

- So what you are **saying** is...
- So your four critical success factors are...?
- So the people involved in the final decision are...?

Closed questions

A closed question usually receives a single word or a short, factual answer. For example, 'Are you hungry?' The answer is Yes or No; 'Where do you work?' The answer is generally the name of the organization and its address.

Closed questions are useful to test your understanding – 'So if the tests on the new product range go well, you would be able to expand internationally?' For frame setting – 'Are you happy with the service you get from your advisors?' And for concluding a discussion or making a decision – 'Do we agree that the best way forward is to schedule a full demonstration?'

Generally the longer the question is, the shorter the answer will be.

All five types of questions are important but some are more powerful than others in helping you to understand another person. The most powerful, Why, How and What, not only help you to understand, they also help your prospect to think about their business in a way they may not have done before. When a client says 'That's a good question' you know you are getting them to think.

FIGURE 8.3 Powerful questions

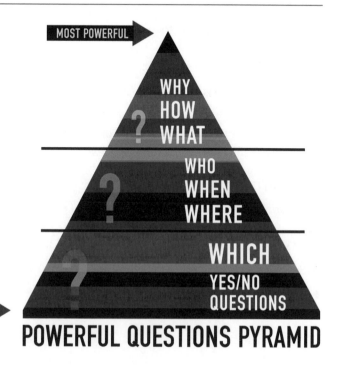

MOST POWERFUL

WHY
HOW
WHAT

WHO
WHEN
WHERE

WHICH
YES/NO
QUESTIONS

LEAST POWERFUL

POWERFUL QUESTIONS PYRAMID

When you use powerful questions in the language and context of your prospect's world then the questions become super powerful. For instance, if you are selling to a professional services firm, you would ask about fee income, not turnover. If you are asking about the future plans of a company, putting it into the context of issues facing their marketplace reinforces your credibility. For example:

- *How will the changes in regulation that come into effect next year affect your European operations?*
- *How has the reduction in government spending on infrastructure affected your growth plans?*
- *How will the recent announcement by the* Financial Industry Regulatory Authority affect you clients?

If you want to win business – shut up!

I don't care how much you know until I know how much you care.

Charles H Green, *The Trusted Advisor*

Actively listening to others is probably the greatest investment that you can make when building long-term trusted relationships. Listening demonstrates that you are interested, and that you care about your client, and it provides evidence of congruency with the Principled Selling approach.

Listening plays a key part in building trust; but how good are you at it really? Most people know that listening is a good thing – but some act as though it's only important when it's other people listening to them!

Principled Selling Tip: Go to **www.principledgroup.com/resources** and try out the online listening assessment.

Listening isn't easy

The most basic of all human needs is the need to understand and be understood. The best way to understand people is to listen to them.

Dr Ralph Nichols, the father of listening

I was speaking with a musician who told me that measures of silence in music are not waiting periods, they are times of active listening, much like a good conversation. With music, silence accentuates listening.

Being quiet is a good start when it comes to listening but too often people are just hearing, not listening. Sometimes there is so much noise going on in our heads that it becomes impossible to be truly silent and listen for words, tone and meaning.

It's worse for those who have a strong opinion or extensive experience. Some people don't even stay quiet long enough to allow the other person to speak and constantly interrupt. Interruptions happen because one party can't wait to get their point or opinion across. When I ask groups what they think of people who have a habit of interrupting they use words like: rude, frustrating, irritating, annoying, self-interested.

The interrupter may think they are getting a point across but more often than not they are simply switching the other person off, or the other person pushes back with their own arguments and no one is listening to anyone.

Listening isn't just about being quiet

Even if interrupting is avoided, the seller might be silent, but often their brain isn't. Their head can be buzzing with thoughts about the next questions to ask, the next point to make, listening for buying signals, wondering if they will make a sale, wondering what's for dinner.

When your brain is active with all this noise it is impossible to effectively listen. Every time you think *I wish he would hurry up* – you miss what he is actually saying. Every time you think *I need this deal* – you miss what is being said. It is not a function of intellect or intelligence. It is simply that the central processing part of the brain can't process what is being said at the same time as forming thoughts.

To listen for understanding you have to be in the moment, to allow the silence to be broken only by the words of the other person. You have to suspend judgement and listen with a clear mind.

If you think about it you pretty much always know when someone isn't listening to you; and prospects and customers know when they are not being listened to. There are dozens of obvious as well as subtle signals that human beings are sensitive to. You notice if someone's eyes glance across the room and they lose attention, you notice when someone asks the same question twice or if someone doesn't take a moment to digest what have said before pouncing on you with their own view. When a prospect starts to believe they are not being genuinely listened to, the dynamics of a meeting change, they fall back to their story of omission and never provide the level of insight needed to win business.

Barriers which prevent you listening

The most common barriers to listening are:

● interests;
● expectations;
● assumptions and past experience.

Interests

If you are not genuinely interested in learning about your prospect's world it will affect listening because you will ask questions only about what interests you. If you are an employment lawyer for instance, there is a risk you will only ask about issues around legal topics that interest you, instead of wider business issues facing the client. In the same way a creative designer might only ask about design instead of how design impacts the clients business.

Expectations

If you have expectations that go beyond building a strong relationship, you risk only listening for pain points or buying signals. Anything else the prospect says will be filtered out as you focus attention on listening for what you hope to hear.

Assumptions and past experience

The two most difficult barriers to overcome are assumptions and past experience. Making assumptions is a human trait and is particularly evident in those of us with years of experience and knowledge. We are experts in our field, have extensive experience of solving customer problems and we might feel we've seen it all, *Been there and got the tee shirt.*

I've even had interesting debates with technical people in professional services and high-tech businesses who have been quite blunt in telling me that as the technical expert they usually know more than the client and can therefore make judgements about what the client needs pretty quickly. One lawyer even tried to convince me that even if others should not assume, his assumptions were safe to make.

The problem is that making assumptions based on past experience kills listening and *not listening* kills relationships.

CASE STUDY

'We recently won a major project to design and build a water treatment plant. Six companies competed for the project, all of them with the ability to provide the right technical solution. *The client said we won the contract because we were good listeners and spent lots of time understanding the importance to the community of this project.* It was always obvious to us that our client needed more than a water-treatment *just* plant; they wanted us to be proactive in the community.

Five major suppliers in the Turkish engineering sector had made the assumption that this project was just about delivering a technical solution. They were wrong but they probably assumed that it was won by the company who offered the lowest price – wrong again. The clients said we were the only company that demonstrated we really understood what they wanted.

Hakan Urey, Country Manager Turkey, pan-European engineering company

Be a good listener. Your ears will never get you in trouble.

Frank Tyger, columnist and humourist

Passive vs active listening skills

With passive listening, you are like a voice recorder. You absorb the information given so long as the speaker provides you with a clear message and makes their delivery interesting enough to keep your attention. Active listening is the process of listening attentively while someone else speaks, reframing and reflecting back what is said, without judgement or advice.

CASE STUDY

'When listening is active, you "get inside" the speaker's head so that you understand the communication from his or her point of view. You have to concentrate, and you have to want to fully understand what the speaker is saying. When you use active listening techniques for an entire meeting you are as tired as the speaker because when it is over you have put as much energy into listening as they have into speaking.'

David Turner, Director, Questas Consulting Ltd

Active listening skills

Eye contact. It is ironic that while you listen with your ears, people judge whether you are listening by looking at your eyes. Making eye contact with the speaker focuses your attention, reduces the likelihood that you'll become distracted, and encourages the speaker.

Affirmations. Nods and appropriate facial expressions provide feedback to the speaker through non verbal signals that show you are interested.

Avoid distractions. Some actions or gestures suggest to the speaker that you are distracted and not listening. Looking at your watch, shuffling papers, playing with your pen, glancing out of a window, or worse, picking up your smart phone all make the speaker feel that you're bored or uninterested.

Ask questions. The active listener analyses what they hear and asks questions to gain clarification, ensure understanding, and to assure the speaker that they are listening.

Reframing. Reframing means restating in your own words what the speaker has said. The effective listener uses phrases such as 'What I hear you saying is...' or 'Do you mean...?' Reframing what has already been said is an excellent control device to check that you are listening carefully. You can't reframe accurately if your mind is wandering or if you are thinking about what you're going to say next. It is also a good control for accuracy. When you reframe using your own words and feedback to the speaker, you confirm the accuracy of your understanding.

Avoid interrupting. Let the speaker complete his or her thoughts before you try to respond. Don't try to second-guess where the speaker's thoughts are going. When the speaker is finished, you'll know.

Don't be afraid of pauses. When the other person pauses it is usually because they are thinking, so when you ask a question be silent and allow the other person time to think. You can also use pauses yourself to evaluate an answer and phrase the next question.

Don't talk over. Most people would rather speak about their own ideas than listen to what someone else says. Too many sellers listen only because it's the price they have to pay to get people to let them speak. While talking might be more fun and silence might be uncomfortable, you can't talk and listen at the same time.

Smooth transitions. In meetings you will be continually shifting back and forth between the roles of speaker and listener. The active listener makes smooth transitions from speaker to listener and back to speaker. From a listening perspective, this means concentrating on what a speaker has to say and not worrying about what you are going to say next.

Summarizing and reflecting. Giving a summary of what a speaker said and which they confirm is totally accurate is active listening nirvana. Summarizing accurately and reflecting on what has been said is the ultimate proof that you are genuinely interested and have understood the speaker.

Explore to guarantee understanding

Getting a full understanding of your potential dream client's world is a bit like oil exploration. To find oil, exploratory drilling starts at the surface using a wide drilling tool until the engineers are sure they have come to the point where the drill has to be changed to advance into more difficult territory. At that point they use an intermediate casing to secure the well before proceeding. The procedure is followed until the next level has been successfully secured and the tool changed again before advancing towards the target – to strike oil.

Oil isn't usually cooperative enough to conveniently lie in one place and therefore exploration companies sink several wells to fully explore an oil field.

When you meet a prospect for the first time your target is to fully understand their needs and wants before moving on to explain how you might be able to help. There will be several specific topics that you will want to ask about and each topic needs to be fully explored before moving to the next. When you use the Principled Selling EXPLORE model you are guaranteed to strike your target – a full understanding of the client's requirements.

The Principled Selling EXPLORE acronym

The EXPLORE acronym provides a useful reminder of how to structure questions in a first meeting:

- **Ex**plain;
- **P**repare;
- **L**isten;
- **O**pen specific;
- **R**eflect and summarize;
- **E**valuate.

Explain

Start by motivating the other person to answer questions as mentioned in Chapter 7, explaining that you would like to understand their organization and then share anything about your products or services that might be useful to them.

Prepare

All you need to prepare in advance of the meeting is one powerful question for each topic you would like to cover. Don't use a list of prepared questions as this can sound more like an interrogation than a meeting to build a relationship and understanding.

For example. If you want to explore your client's future growth plans, prepare a question such as *'What are your future growth plans?'* The answer you get will provide plenty of opportunities to ask more specific questions.

Always start with the most powerful questions first: Tell me..., Explain to me..., Describe to me..., Why..., How... and What...

Listen

Use active listening. Your next question is derived from the answer they give to your prepared open questions.

Open specific

Use open specific questions to explore answers in more detail.

FIGURE 8.4   Explore to fully understand

FIGURE 8.5 Topics to explore

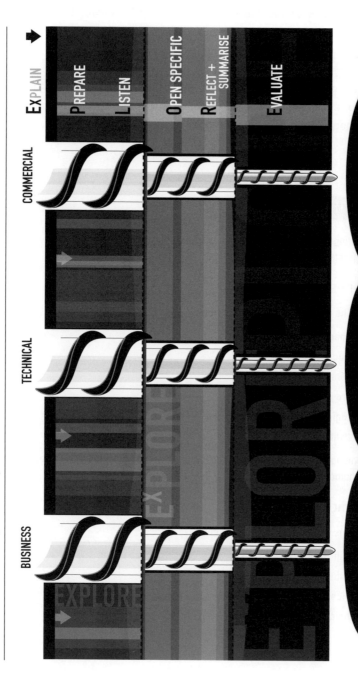

Reflect and summarize

Use closed questions to check and confirm understanding. Don't move on to another topic until you have fully explored the current one.

Evaluate

When you have covered all the topics you want to explore, assess the relevance and importance of the information you have received before moving on to the Explain stage of the E^3 meeting model.

Planning the topics to explore

E^3 meetings have three main topics to explore. Business, Technical and Commercial.

Business topics

Questions around business topics cover:

- Company history;
- Products or services;
- Current situation;
- Future plans;
- Stategic direction;
- Motivations.

Depending on your own market sector, questions might include vision, leadership, management, culture and people.

Technical topics

Questions around technical topics cover:

- specific projects;
- specifications;
- service levels;
- technical requirements.

Commercial topics

Questions around commercial topics cover:

- budgets and money;
- the basis on which any decision would be made;
- the decision making process;
- timing;
- competitors;
- alternatives;
- current suppliers;
- critical success factors driving the decision.

Even professional salespeople sometimes fail to explore the commercial topics fully. The more answers you have about the commercial topics, the stronger your qualification of the opportunity will be. For instance it isn't safe to assume that only one person will be involved in decision making, that they can afford you or that their time frame is the same as yours.

Principled Selling Tip: Never assume you know the answers to commercial questions – always ask.

Topic hopping

However well you guide a meeting it sometimes you will start to explore one topic but before you have fully understood the prospect will hop to another. It often happens when you get someone to really think about their business; new topics pop into their mind as they describe their world. The best way to deal with this is to follow where they go, explore and go back later to the previous topic.

Don't think transactional and don't win small

If your product or service is complex, and a long-term project is involved or a product demonstration is needed, it is highly unlikely that you will walk out with an order after one hour. There may be rare occasions when a requirement is so urgent and you have built so much trust through your M2M marketing that the prospect wants to do business with you immediately. Even if you face one those rare occasions, stop and think.

When you are evaluating the best way forward don't think just one transaction ahead or your customers will think the same way as well. Forget 'a bird in the hand' theory and think lifetime value. Ask yourself what the dream client could be worth to you and your business if you secure a long-term relationship where they buy and re-buy across your full range of products and services.

Closing doesn't form part of the Principled Selling vocabulary because it suggests gimmicks designed to elicit a decision in the seller's time frame. The risk with closing is that you fail to be congruent with the approach you have taken in the meeting so far – building a trusted relationship. In an attempt to win a transaction now, even if the prospect says *yes*, they are more likely to think transactionally too. Winning small with a dream client at a first meeting probably means you will soon be out looking for the next dream client to win small with.

Principled Selling Tip: Explore business, technical and commercial topics in full before moving on to the Explain stage of the E^3 meeting model.

Add value and explain a way forward

When you have evaluated what you have heard it is time for you to speak about ways in which you might be able to help. As you do this you should be adding real value. Keep the valuable content theme going by giving something free. That might be free advice on the spot, something you could offer to send after the meeting or explaining how you helped another client in a similar situation.

The way forward

As the meeting comes towards the end of the allotted time it is really important to get commitment from the prospect about the best way forward.

Depending on your type of business the way forward following a first meeting might include:

- scheduling a further meeting;
- agreeing to keep in touch;
- finding another prospect.

You might decide when you are evaluating that you need a further meeting to gain more insight, to meet other people or to go back with some ideas after you have had time to relect. Taking time to reflect is very powerful. It demonstrates that you want to take a considered approach and gives you an opportunity to think about how to win a customer for life.

Getting a commitment to the way forward has to involve the prospect taking action. That action might be fixing a date there and then or agreeing that you call at a specific time the next day to arrange the next meeting.

If there is no opportunity in the near future to do business but you would like to keep in touch; get commitment that it is OK for you to continue to send valuable content and to make a catch-up call in three months' time.

You could find a another prospect by asking for a referral. You have built credibility and trust, so asking for a referral wouldn't seem unusual. Just ask *'Is there anyone else in your organization or do you have any contacts that you think might find our service useful?'*

Sometimes you are going to find that the prospect you thought would be a dream client is actually not someone you would want to do business with. It's an extreme example but recently an accountant told me this happened to her when it was obvious the potential dream client was a crook!

On the other hand you might be asked to put something in writing, prepare a proposal or make a presentation. These are covered in detail in Chapter 9 where you will also find out how to convince your dream client that they want to buy from you!

Summary

Avoid premature presentations by first seeking to understand your prospect. You build trust when you demonstrate genuine interest and when you invest time to fully understand your potential customer's requirements. Everyone has their 'story of omission'; the surface level information they will freely share with anyone who asks. Real insight comes from getting below the iceberg to uncover wants as well as needs. Needs are easy to communicates, wants are emotionally based and more difficult for a prospect to share. The skills used in selling are used instinctively by most people every day; powerful questions and active listening take communication skills to the level of unconscious competence. The most difficult communication skill is listening because interests, expectations, assumptions and past experience get in the way. The EXPLORE model helps you to structure a conversation in a way that guarantees that you will understand the customer, gain insight into their needs and wants, and find the best way forward following the face-to-face meeting.

Action points

- Pick your top five existing customers, working though them one by one, identify their needs and wants.

- Construct one open question for each topic you want to explore in advance of your next meeting. Then watch how much additional infromation flows as the meeting progresses.

- Ask people who know you and who you trust if you are a good listener. If they say *no,* ask for some specific examples to help you. Ask them to watch over you for the next few months as you try to change your behaviour.

- Ask the same people if you have a tendency to 'pounce'. Again ask for specific exmples, and if it is a behaviour you need to focus on, ask someone to watch over you as you try to change.

- Take the online listening assessment at **www.principledgroup.com/resources**

CHAPTER 9

PROPOSALS AND PRESENTATIONS THAT WOW!

You have invested in M2M marketing and the M2B meeting approach in order to build a trusted relationship and to earn the right to tell your story. There will have been times when you have realized quite early in a meeting that you really do have something to offer but you have bitten your tongue until you fully understood your named prospect's requirement. Now it's your turn to explain how you might help and to continue motivating your prospect.

Topics covered in this chapter

- Strategic thinking to win more business
- Proposals that sell and presentations that 'WOW'!
- The Principled Selling way to deal with 'objections'
- Staying confident about your prices or fees

Strategic thinking to win more business

As you quickly evaluate the information you have taken on board at the Explore stage, you should also decide on your best strategy for winning business. Is it your best strategy to carry on now and explain in detail how you could help or do you really need time to reflect and prepare a tailored presentation, proposal or demonstration? Do you have all the information you need and do you have the answers to the commercial questions that influence a decision? Should you suggest meeting other members of the decision making team?

The previous chapter closed with some suggestions about how a relationship might progress following an E³ meeting. In fact sometimes the meeting you had scheduled for an hour runs on because you have done such a good job of building trust that the prospect is motivated to carry on beyond the allotted time. If extra time isn't available, never try to squeeze a full presentation about how you can help in the last five minutes. By all means demonstrate your confidence that you have a solution that can help them and maybe give an example of how you helped customers in similar situation, but don't give in to any pressure you feel to make a premature presentation.

Put that in writing

Any seasoned salesperson will have countless examples of being asked *to put that in writing* at the end of a first meeting. They will also tell you how they promised to get that something in writing back within a couple of days and then burned the midnight oil to put together a detailed proposal for a 'hot' prospect. Many will also tell you they never heard from or spoke to that prospect again, let alone won any business from them. The hot prospect eventually becomes someone to be chased or put on a database.

The main reason this can happen is that if you leave suggestions about the way forward to the prospect, putting it all in writing will seem the most natural and the easiest next step; it is almost the default position. When salespeople get things very wrong it is the prospect's way of politely ending a meeting, knowing that they don't intend to buy or even to read the proposal.

It could also be that they want something to show to other people who will be involved in making a decision. Problems arise if you then depend on the proposal to maintain their motivation or for them to use to motivate their colleagues. No one on the customer's team can ever be as good as you at putting over how you can help them achieve their objectives.

Dealing with formal RFPs (requests for proposals) is different; I have something to say on that later in this chapter.

Principled Selling Tip: Lead the meeting and keep a light-touch control by suggesting the best way forward before you are asked to 'put that in writing'.

As you evaluate your options for moving forward it is important to be realistic about the prospect's decision making process. Depending on what is being purchased, or the value, even the most senior executives are likely to want to discuss any proposal with colleagues. During the explore stage of the E^3 meeting you will have identified the people who influence a decision and as part of your strategy you might need to think about what other relationships you need to develop within the named prospect.

Proposals and presentations that help you win business are those that the prospect helps you to prepare and that talk about what Andy Bounds, in his book *The Jelly Effect*, calls the 'afters'.

When a prospect is motivated to buy from you they will give you advice on how best to structure a proposal or presentation for them. They will advise you about different personalities and how best to motivate them, or at least how not to irritate them. For instance, some people like masses of detail, others like information delivered to them in bullet points. Some people expect a formal slide presentation; others hate them with a passion. The more intelligence you can gather at the first meeting, the better your proposal or presentation will be.

Sell holes not drills

Afters are what a prospect gets after they do business with you. As Richard Denny says, *'No one wants a drill, they want a hole.'* Despite that wisdom many proposals and presentations are full of descriptions of a seller's equivalent of the drill. What people buy is the benefits they get from doing business with you. In crowded marketplaces you have to be sure about what the benefits will be for your prospect.

CASE STUDY

'After once having the market to ourselves, there are now several competitors who can provide the same technology we do for steel rolling mills. In China we see new competitors appearing every year. Customers have to feel that they get more than the technology from us. The way we do business, the way we sell and our ethical culture helps, but most important is showing that we know the issues facing particular customers better than anyone else does and how your solution matches all their requirements better than the competition.'

Neil Fletcher, Product Sales Manager, global metal technologies company

Ultimately most outcomes are related to reducing a risk, increasing revenue or profit, reducing costs, saving time or reducing stress.

When someone buys a computer system they are buying the outcomes that they specifically want. A CRM (customer relationship management) system isn't bought for ease of input, clever software or a customer contact system; those are features. A CRM system might be bought to improve customer service by one client and to sell more to existing customers by another.

When a client instructs an accountant they don't buy technical expertise, they buy peace of mind that regulations have been complied with or that they make a tax saving. Their desired outcomes might be being able to focus more on their core business, make an investment or take a vacation with the tax they save. Salespeople and technicians tend to focus too much on *how* they will deliver a solution rather than what the prospect will gain when they become a buying customer. In other words they provide a presentation full of features rather than benefits.

In a written proposal or a presentation you have to be able to say with certainty that you can provide the desired outcomes *and* provide evidence that proves you will.

Principled Selling Tip: It is the evidence you provide to prove you can deliver the desired outcomes plus your enthusiasm that will convince and WOW the named prospect.

In a proposal or presentation, for each requirement:

- restate the requirement;
- set out your solution and why it will help;
- provide evidence that you can deliver.

For each requirement that your prospect has, your proposal and presentation should specifically demonstrate you have understood, not only the requirements but why they are important. For every requirement you need to demonstrate how your solution will help and then provide evidence to prove you can deliver. Always check that your prospect is happy with your understanding, solution and evidence before moving on to the next requirement.

Examples of evidence

- Case studies
- Written testimonials
- Video testimonials
- Live demonstration

- Customer survey feedback
- Offers of site visits
- Trial products
- Samples

Principled Selling Tip: Case studies and testimonials should talk about measurable results and what was achieved after doing business with you, not just say what a nice bunch of people you are.

Writing a good proposal is an art. The general rule is to make sure it is tailored to what you learned during the E^3 meeting and not to throw in lots of extra unwanted features to pad it out. You should never be afraid of price nor try to hide it; the important thing is to make sure you present it correctly and use the right words. 'Price' or 'fee' can have negative connotations and suggests cost, whereas using the word 'investment' is more positive and suggests outcomes and returns.

You can put a huge amount of effort into a proposal only to find that when it hits the prospect's desk the first page they go to is the one that sets out fees or prices. If cost is sitting there on the page 'naked' there is a risk the recipient will not link what they get for their investment and the benefits with the price or fee you quote. You might have produced a brilliant 20-page proposal but only one page gets looked at. There is a great opportunity to remind the prospect on the investment page about the outcomes they can expect from doing business with you. Rather than let the price or fee sit there naked on the page, surround it by what they will get for their investment.

> ### The benefits sandwich
>
> Everything the customer gets for their investment
>
> £ THE INVESTMENT $
>
> All the benefits and outcomes from doing business with you

Formal RFPs (requests for proposals)

In some sectors the documents you submit will need to be a formal response to an invitation to tender or a request for a proposal. If you apply Principled Selling thinking to a formal process you will have a competitive advantage.

Government, public sector and increasingly larger organizations depend on formal procurement processes to purchase goods and services. Each organization and jurisdiction has it's own rules and regulations that need to be adhered to. Principled Sellers comply with all the ethical demands made by a formal procurement procedure – there are no shortcuts or tricks when it comes to complying with the legal and regulatory requirements demanded. Not only is attempting to take shortcuts not congruent with the Principled Selling approach, it can lead to serious consequences. Some proposals are extremely complex and expert teams are needed to work on them. However, compliance isn't enough.

CASE STUDY

'A RFP is like an exam, you have to hit the pass mark or your proposal will fail. For some reason suppliers insist on submitting proposals right at the last minute and some miss the deadline because of silly mistakes like e-mailing files that are so large they take forever to download. Being even a minute late is like turning up to the examination hall when the door has been locked.'

Simon Richardson, Procurement Manager, Devon and Somerset Fire Service

The minimum you need to be considered is to comply with the terms of the RFP. However, the winning proposal needs to do more than just comply. Before you submit a document check that you have:

- invested considerable time in understanding the client, the key contacts and their world;
- met with key influencers and decision makers;
- understood the strengths and weaknesses of the incumbent supplier;
- tested your ideas with a key contact so that they have been part of formulating the ideal solution.

Then make sure your proposal:

- fully complies with the RFP;
- complies with file size demands for downloads;
- answers all the questions;
- if asked for a detailed response, give a detailed response, particularly to the questions carrying the highest scores;
- contains content that reflects an understanding of the client or customer that goes beyond what is written in the RFP;
- demonstrates that you fully appreciate the client's issues, problems, and challenges to overcome;
- sets out a superior solution for meeting the customer's requirements;
- offers a competitive advantage over your competition;
- includes contract terms that are acceptable to the customer;
- clearly articulates reasons why the customer should select you;
- contains highly relevant testimonials and case studies;
- contains evidence of your competence;
- has excellent visual layout and graphics;
- contains pricing that is within the client's range of acceptability **and** that meets your own revenue and profit goals;
- **arrives before the deadline.**

Increasing your conversion rate

Probably the single biggest mistake organizations make is to put a huge effort into proposals they know they are not going to win. I have met dozens of individuals in major organizations who have told me that their conversion rate is appallingly low and that they regularly invest time and resources into putting forward proposals that they stand no chance of winning.

The most effective thing you can do to increase your conversion rate is to submit fewer proposals. Having a bid/no bid mechanism is vital. Just like when you chose selection criteria for named prospects, you can establish criteria for which RFPs you will respond to. The next most important thing is to really understand the client's requirements and build a relationship – long before a formal proposal is requested.

CASE STUDY

'Most organizations know that they have to comply with the formal requirements of an RFP. You don't have a chance if you can't get that part right. On the other hand the main reason for losing a bid is lacking a full understanding of the potential client's requirements. An invitation to tender gives everyone the same information to respond to, it has to be a level playing field. Sometimes meetings with procurement are allowed to find out more, sometimes not. The bids we tend to win are those where we understand what the client wants better than our competitors do.'

Darren Laurie, Account Exec, Atos SA

Once a formal request is issued, there are few chances to build a relationship that will give you a deeper understanding of the potential customer. If those potential clients who request proposals are already on your named prospect list you will have spent time getting to know them long before they go out to tender for the products or services you supply. It isn't surprising that most RFPs are won by the incumbent provider – they usually know the client better than anyone.

You can apply the Principled Selling Growth Model to opportunities requiring formal proposals in exactly the same way as any other named prospect in your target market.

Making memorable presentations

I deliberately avoid using the word 'pitch' – even though it is commonly used to describe telling the story about you, your company, and what you do. Making a pitch suggests something you do to an audience and something that is all about you. On the good side, pitch suggests energy and enthusiasm, and

I certainly advocate plenty of that when it is your turn to tell your story. Making a presentation memorable is about great content that is communicated by the right people in the right way.

Put your best team forward

Sometimes you may have no choice about who makes the presentation. If you are in business as a freelance or otherwise on your own, you might be the chief cook and bottle washer. Even so think carefully about who you could include in your presentation team. The best team is made up of those people most likely to engage with the personalities of the decision makers and who have the right knowledge and skills. If you are fielding a team, you shouldn't automatically take those colleagues who might be available on the day or those who think they have a right to be there because of seniority. If you do work on your own consider taking along a supplier, strategic partner or maybe a customer who could add weight to your presentation.

Plan and rehearse

Presentations that WOW are always planned and rehearsed. Time is at a premium for everyone these days but time invested before a presentation increases your chance of winning. Never churn out a standard presentation hoping that it will fit the audience.

CASE STUDY

'I was in the Ukraine recently as part of a team giving the usual technical presentation that we tend to give all over the world. After 45 minutes an engineer in the audience said "Yes, we know all that from your competitors who do the same, what do you bring that is new?" It proved to me that having a fantastic technical solution isn't good enough any more.'

Neil Fletcher, Product Sales Manager, global metal industries company

Remember that everyone you present to is interested in outcomes. Use part of your presentation to provide the reassurances needed to prove your competence but spend most of the time ensuring you convey your understanding of the particular customer by fully answering the questions you were asked to address.

If you are selective in answering the questions you were asked to cover in the presentation, you will fail.

There is never time to include everything you could say, so prepare three powerful messages that you would like your audience to remember after you present and then rehearse, rehearse, rehearse.

WOW the audience

The most common statement a procurement professional writes after seeing a presentation is *'failed to convey confidence'*. As Simon Richardson of Devon and Somerset Fire Service said to me: 'The first part of the examination was passed and the presentation team let themselves down by giving a poor presentation.'

Presentations that WOW are those where the team focuses on the audience, on benefits, on outcomes – and on speaking well.

The best speakers are:

- interesting;
- enthusiastic;
- knowledgeable;
- credible;
- engaging;
- natural;
- clearly spoken;
- well prepared.

Being enthusiastic about doing business with a prospect is demonstrated by the words you use and your voice – you don't have to wave your arms around and be highly animated. You can be interesting as well as being grounded, providing all the gravitas needed in any situation. However, serious doesn't have to be boring.

I once engaged a law firm because one of the partners told me they would *love* to work with us. All the firms we looked at could do the technical work, but it was only one which used any emotional connection or enthusiasm with us in their presentation.

Principled Selling tip: make sure all your team, however technically qualified they might be, can engage an audience.

Don't get bogged down with 'objections'

Resistance not objections

No matter how good your proposal or presentation, there will be times when you are asked questions or challenged about your solution. In old-style traditional selling these questions were called objections and salespeople were taught objection-handling techniques based on over-complex mnemonics to remind them how to deal with them. One sales training company working with professional services firms in the UK has a ten-letter mnemonic they ask their trainees to remember. As Richard Denny, author of *Selling to Win,* says 'A disproportionate amount of importance is given to handling objections'. I agree with Richard and prefer to think of questions and challenges as *resistance.*

It is totally normal for someone considering buying from you to ask questions and challenge you. It is their duty to do the best for their organization and they may have to justify their decision to colleagues, superiors or shareholders.

It is really important to regard resistance as interest, not push back. If you are being asked questions and challenged the prospect is engaging with you. Your job is to deal with the resistance effectively and professionally. Don't get defensive and never argue. Even if you win an argument a prospect can vote with their chequebook to ensure you are the ultimate loser.

Is it a condition?

A condition is a genuine non-negotiable reason that a prospect cannot do business with you right now. Examples of non-negotiable reasons might be:

- They have no money.
- The timing is wrong.
- There are existing contractual commitments.

If they have no money, that is a straightforward situation to deal with. Go back if and when they can afford you. Timing might be down to change in management, a takeover, a merger or something else outside their control. Existing contractual commitments can't be ignored and Principled Sellers work with prospects to make sure they don't breach covenants.

Usually only a very small number of conditions exist. Most of the questions or challenges you get will be about your ability to match the named prospect's requirements, technical specifications and service issues. Most of the resistance you could get is eliminated by your careful choice of named prospect.

Handling resistance

Just because you are told your prospect has no budget or can't afford your solution doesn't mean they have no money or discretionary power to move budgets around. When someone says *It's too expensive* they might mean:

- I have no money.
- I don't have the budget signed off.
- You are more expensive than our current supplier.
- It's not my decision.
- It's my job to negotiate the price down.
- I would like a discount.
- It's more than I thought.

You have to find out what the prospect means before you can provide a satisfactory response.

Handle resistance with this simple 5-Step PECAN approach:

- Pause
- Explore
- Confirm understanding
- Address all concerns and issues
- Next step.

Pause

Resistance isn't a personal attack on you, your company or your products or services, so when you are questioned or challenged pause and stay relaxed. The pause will demonstrate that you are reflecting on what has been said and you will avoid jumping in with a defensive comment. Take care that your body language doesn't change to suggest that you have been riled; don't suddenly shift about in your seat or sit forward as if going in to attack. It will signal that you are uncomfortable and can escalate the most innocent of questions into a major issue.

Explore

The most important thing to do is to understand in full what you are being asked or what the challenge is. Use the questioning and listening skills you learned about in Chapter 7 to fully explore any resistance.

Confirm understanding

After you have summarized to the satisfaction of the prospect what they are really saying and before you provide your answer check to see if there are any more questions or challenges. You could spend time responding to one comment only to find that when you have answered that there are two or three other challenges to follow. It is best to get those challenges on to the table at this stage and explore them before moving forward.

Address all concerns and issues

Once you are sure you have understood any resistance then provide your best answer. You might be able to satisfy all points there and then or you may need to reflect and get back to the prospect on more complex challenges.

Next step

When you have addressed all concerns and issues, suggest the next step to move things forward. Make sure you get agreement and if this involves a further meeting, get the date scheduled while you are in front of the prospect.

Handling the price or fee challenge

When I work with groups the most common questions I am asked about resistance is being challenged on price. You read above some of the reasons a prospect might say you are too expensive and of course you need to find out the real reason. The reality is that sellers often have a bigger hang-up about price than the potential customer does.

It's a confidence thing

Handling prices or fees is all about your confidence. You will always have price or fee challenges if you are not 100 per cent confident that your product or service is worth what you ask. Sometimes whole sales forces catch what Richard Denny refers to as 'priceitis'.

CASE STUDY

'Feedback from the front-line salespeople was that they were not hitting sales targets because our products were too expensive. It spread like wild fire across the whole sales force in Australia. We responded by telling some regions that they could sell at any price they thought that they could get for a period of three months. Sales stayed the same. We knew it wasn't price that was the problem but needed to prove it to the sales teams.'

Tony McCormack, Country Manager Australia, leading Japanese photocopier manufacturer

If it were true that people only buy on price then the best selling smart phone (Apple iphone) would be the cheapest, as would the best-selling car (Toyota Corolla) and in both cases the cheapest clearly are not the top sellers. Buyers actually make decisions based on value for money, not price. Only when a product is truly a commodity in the mind of the customer (their perception is that they can get *exactly* the same product or service from lots of providers) does a buyer use price as the deciding factor.

How individuals perceive value for money varies enormously. In the Netherlands recently I asked 10 people to write down the cost of:

- a very expensive watch you could buy at Schiphol Airport;
- a very expensive property in Amsterdam;
- a very expensive holiday to the USA.

From people in the same room I got a range of prices from €800 to €20,000 for an expensive watch; from €500,000 to €5m for an expensive property and from €4,000 to €10,000 for an expensive holiday. Value is in the eyes of the beholder and is dependent upon their expectations.

The problem is that if you don't see the value in your solution you can guarantee that no prospect ever will. If you are not confident you will be giving out signals by what you say, how you say it and through your body language. Your confidence about your pricing makes a huge difference. For instance, a commercial real estate negotiator I was asked to coach, had the habit of swallowing hard after setting out pricing details of optional extras and saying *'does that work for you?'* Those five words and his lack of confidence always kept the negotiation going and he always gave more money away. He gave less money away when he simply stayed calm and said *'which options do you prefer'*?

What you say and how you say it will signal how confident you are and how open you are to negotiation. Never try to sell anything that you don't believe in and that you don't believe offers good value to your prospect.

Never be afraid of price; your confidence will shine through and add to your credibility.

Principled price negotiation

When you use M2M marketing and M2B skills and behaviours your named prospect will be motivated to buy from you before price comes on to the agenda. Psychologically the prospect will have made the decision to do business with you but, as mentioned above, price might be a point of negotiation. In many cases, if you have built relationships using the Principled Selling approach, the price you quote will be accepted without challenge.

The objective of Principled Price Negotiation is to ensure that both buyer and seller leave the table feeling comfortable with what has been agreed. There is a risk of buyer's remorse if a seller uses tricks like false deadlines, long waiting lists, low stock levels or other pressure to close a deal at a price that the prospect isn't really happy with. Equally, if the seller walks away unhappy there is a risk of resentment that can affect service levels and long-term relationships.

If your price or fee is challenged with the words *It's too expensive* – simply ask *Compared to what?*

The response might be:

- *Compared to what I was expecting.*
- *Compared to another quote I have.*
- *Compared to my budget.*

You should then ask: *By how much?*

The key rule is not to try to justify the full price or fee you are asking, just to justify the *difference* between their expectation and your price.

If total fees for consultancy advice for instance was $100,000 and the buyer said they had a budget of $90,000, all you need to find justification for is the $10,000 difference.

Whatever you do don't make it easy by crumbling on price immediately. If you do you will lose credibility because the prospect will first ask themselves why you over-quoted in the first place and then will try to knock you down even further because you give in so easily.

Never discount!

When you start to discount your price in a negotiation the prospect will naturally push to see how much more discount they can get – particularly if you discount easily. If you really can't justify the price difference, and the named prospect won't move, then you have to change the offer before you change the price if you are to maintain credibility.

The words to remember under these circumstances are *If you... then I...*

For example:

If you could second someone from your team to write the staff survey, then I might be able to match your budget.

or

If you can make an advance payment of 50 per cent then I could match the competitor's quote.

or

If you can delay the start of the project until our quiet period, then I could possibly match the price you expected.

If you have to change your price, then change the offer.

Don't be afraid to ask for the order

When you follow the Principled Selling approach, the energy and motivation to buy will come from your prospect.

Moving to confirming the go ahead, signing an order or engagement agreement is just the next natural step in the process. Often the prospect will be asking you what they need to do to next.

Sometimes you need to continue your light-touch control. At the appropriate time and when you have ensured the prospect is totally satisfied with the solution you have put forward, don't be afraid to say *'All we need to do now is complete the paperwork'* or something similar.

Be persistent but never chase

If you have been involved in winning business you will know that there are times when you have had a great meeting, the named prospect was really enthusiastic and you left with a good feeling that this opportunity would turn into a sale. Maybe a great proposal or presentation followed and the feeling that the order was in the bag was so strong that the figures were written into the sales forecast for the next month.

Then a couple of weeks went by and the expected order didn't materialize. A call to the prospect resulted in assurances that everything was fine, but there was no order yet. The forecast was amended to show the sale would now be *next month*. The boss probably said at this stage you should make sure you keep on top of things and *chase up the order*. A few phone calls and a few weeks later, despite chasing there was still no order. It's at this point I've too often observed a shift in the attitude of the salesperson. If a call or two to the buyer isn't returned, suddenly it's the prospect's fault that the sales forecast has to be amended again. Suddenly the prospect, the potential dream client is being accused in sales meetings of being a time waster. Further e-mails and phone calls go unanswered. The boss asks if this piece of business is ever going to be *closed* and somehow your calls still stay unanswered.

The prospect controls the timing

I learned a long time ago is that the potential customer controls the timing of when they buy. If pressure is used to try and speed up decision making it can have exactly the opposite effect of what was intended.

Let's assume you do go away from first meetings with all the right information and with as many of the commercial qualification questions answered as possible (the more we can answer the stronger the potential for a positive decision), you also need to bear in mind that when you leave, your potential customer goes back to their real-world day job of multiple and conflicting priorities.

Most customers aren't being rude or discourteous when they don't respond to follow up calls; they are just saying it's not their priority right now. It isn't our job to make what we want them to do their priority; it's up to us to make sure they are just as enthusiastic to buy from us when the time is right for them.

Don't interrupt

If you are not careful there is a risk that your follow-up calls can end up being an interruption of the prospect's day rather than a help. Follow-up calls and voicemail messages end up feeling like chasing – which feels like pressure – which feels uncomfortable and which can end up with the potential customer avoiding you. You do need to keep in touch and show interest of course, otherwise they may become more enthusiastic about buying from a competitor.

We already know from Chapter 5 on valuable content that if any follow-up becomes a negative experience or ends up with the potential customer feeling that they were sent something generic or inappropriate, then their enthusiasm for you takes a nosedive, more quickly than if you had made no contact at all.

The right thing to do is ensure that any contact you make offers real value. With careful thought any follow-up can ensure that there is a reason to make contact that isn't experienced as an interruption to the day in pursuit of a buying decision, but as something that adds to your potential customers' day. This is unlikely to be a newsletter, brochure or other device which shows that they have merely been put onto a database. It will be valuable and appropriate content which will be useful and interesting. This will ensure that over time enthusiasm is maintained. If you are tempted to chase for a decision or an order, stop and think:

- Might there be something going on in the customer's world right now that has higher priority?
- How can I make contact and add value?
- How can I maintain enthusiasm to buy my product or service – when the time is right?

Principled Selling Tip: Drop the word chase from your selling vocabulary – always think follow-up and valuable content.

Summary

Think strategically about how to win a long-term relationship with every named prospect. Consider all the factors that are specific to the particular situation and how best to win a customer for life. Make sure you focus on benefits and outcomes in your proposals and presentations, provide evidence and remember that formal RFPs are usually won because of the time invested in understanding the customer, not the time invested in producing the formal documentation. Deliver presentations that WOW by ensuring the right people deliver the right content in the right way. Forget about 'objection handling' and deal with questions and challenges as resistance that show interest and don't be defensive. Finally, stay confident about your price or fee; never discount and change the offer if you need to change the price.

Action points

- List the most common benefits and outcomes your customers gain from doing business with you.
- Check your proposals and presentations to ensure they are tailored to each customers required outcomes.

- Invest time early in understanding the world of potential dream clients who will use formal RFPs.

- Practise with colleagues, using the five-step PECAN approach dealing with the typical questions or challenges you get.

- Practise principled price negotiation with colleagues.

CHAPTER 10

PRINCIPLED SELLING KEY ACCOUNT MANAGEMENT

In Chapter 9 we completed the 'Motivate' section of the Principled Selling Growth Model and you are now fully prepared to win more business – great news! In this chapter we will look at how taking the Principled Selling approach to key account management will strengthen and grow the relationships you work hard to win.

Topics covered in this chapter

- Making the commitment
- Securing existing customer relationships
- Securing and developing key account relationships
- Key account management – action plan

CASE STUDY

'Somewhere today a competitor is planning to take your dream clients away from you. If you want to avoid always chasing new customers you have to secure current relationships and create new opportunities. You and your company have to be fully committed to Principled Selling key account management.'

Darren Laurie, Client Exec, Atos SA

Making the commitment

Key account management is not about having differing levels of service for different customers. It isn't a choice between gold, silver or bronze levels of service. It isn't about getting a greater share of the clients' wallet.

Principled Selling key account management is about having a proactive plan to:

- strengthen existing relationships to secure your customers from competitive incursion;
- develop new relationships which lead to opportunities for increased revenue;
- help your customers to be more successful.

Getting key account management right, getting it better than your competitors undoubtedly requires commitment. Many organizations say that key account management is both important and difficult and they are right. As one sales leader put it in an online discussion group, *'It is hard making key account management happen in our business. I can see all the opportunity – more sales, better profit, sustained growth and better relationships – but all that some of my senior colleagues seem to see is cost, service problems and risk.'*

Before setting out to make Principled Selling account management work for you, be sure that there is commitment and support at the most senior level in your organization. When the business owner, CEO or senior C-suite executives are leading by example and demonstrating that key account management is important by supporting the implementation of action plans, you can be sure others in the organization will follow. The benefits of getting it right far outweigh the investment.

You can massively differentiate your business from your competitors' by taking a Principled Selling approach to key account management; but you do have to think long term. After all, even if you are under pressure to meet short-term financial performance, the customers that generate profit for you don't think short term about the benefits they plan to get from doing business with you.

Like all things Principled Selling, commitment to key account management must include being genuinely interested in the value your customers get from doing business with you.

CASE STUDY

'Having a Principled Selling key account action plan and implementing it has proved invaluable in propelling our business forward in terms of increased sales productivity. It has had a measurable impact on our business results.'

Mark Bradley, Sales Director, international life assurance company

When you consider the benefits it is ironic that many suppliers instigate key account management as a response to customer demand rather than implementing it proactively. Whatever the size of your organization, if you have key accounts that you would lose sleep over if you lost them, you need to manage them just as well as you manage winning new business.

Securing existing customer relationships

When the customer service you provide is congruent with the Principled Selling approach, customers and clients stay with you, buy more from you and refer you to other potential customers.

Customers and clients who receive Principled Selling customer service:

- agree to exclusive long-term relationships with you;
- will pay a premium for the products and services you provide;
- are more cost effective for you to serve;
- refer you to other potential customers;
- are motivated to buy more from you;
- are advocates who publicly support you;
- provide honest and valuable feedback;
- are more forgiving when you get it wrong;
- generate more profit for you.

Managing customers' experiences

You have probably heard of CRM (customer relationship management). When I first worked with clients on customer service projects over 15 years ago, CRM systems seemed to be the answer to everyone's customer service issues. Quite quickly organizations found that a CRM system not only didn't fire the imagination of their own sales teams, it certainly didn't WOW customers to know they were on a customer database, however sophisticated.

A perennial problem with CRM systems is that front-line account managers and sales people often don't use them. The head of marketing in a commercial property firm told me that they had made a huge financial investment in a bespoke software solution that after one year only contained name and address information about clients and almost zero information about prospects. Front-line people were just not providing information or interacting with the system. Why? Because no front-line person saw any benefit for them or their clients.

A CRM system is great at churning data and can be a vital tool, but it adds little or nothing to the experience clients and customers get of doing business with you. In some cases it even detracts from a positive experience.

CASE STUDY

'I have a problem with the whole idea of 'managing' a client relationship. 'Things' can be managed: computers, buildings, systems, car fleets, etc, where control of the asset is important. Relationships with people, however, tend not to thrive when one party thinks that the relationship can be managed.

'I know we can't manage customers but we can manage their experience of doing business with us. We have full control over the level of service our client's experience.'

Richard Wylie, CEO, Principled Group Ltd

'Satisfied' customers are just not good enough

Client and customer loyalty can't be taken for granted. Even if the supply of your product or service has been carried out effectively and efficiently, you can't *expect* loyalty. Customers measure suppliers not on what they *say* about service but what they *do*.

When an organization under-delivers on a client's expectations, the result is a dissatisfied client. Dissatisfied customers sometimes become high maintenance due to the level of complaints, or, worse, they never tell you they are unhappy. They are the worst type of nice customer.

Letter from a nice customer

I am a nice customer, you all know me. I'm the one who never complains, no matter what kind of service I get.

If I call a service line, press all the right keys and get disconnected in the process or made to wait ten minutes to speak to a human being, I'm patient and don't complain. When my call is answered within three rings but I get a snooty person who tells me I got through to the wrong department, I don't respond by being rude in return – I just hang up and try another number.

When a supplier says that they are having a few staffing problems (again) and they are sorry that the project will be delayed by another few days, I thank them for letting me know, not bothering to point out that their problem has become my problem and I now have to find a way to avoid letting my own customers down.

If a salesperson, an account manager, my lawyer or my accountant is late for a meeting and blames the traffic, public transport or being busy, I don't bother to point out that traffic and public transport is always unpredictable and maybe they could set out a bit earlier, or tell them that I'm busy too.

I never criticise, I never moan, I'm not the sort to make a scene if I get poor service in a restaurant, at a bank or in a store. Not me – I'm a nice customer.

When you push me too far I just take my business elsewhere, where they are smart enough to recruit and train people who appreciate nice customers. The world is full of nice customers who laugh at all your expensive promotions and marketing to get me to buy more or to attract new customers when all you needed to do was give good service, some kind words and maybe even a smile. If your sales are down, if your people find it hard to hit their sales target or if customers are moving their loyalty to your competitors remember people like me.

Signed,

All the nice customers who never complain and never come back.

No customer is going to stay loyal to a supplier or advisor who under-delivers on their promises. It's not a business model that will sustain profitable growth.

CASE STUDY

'Our CEO tells a salutary tale about a major client won many years ago who three months after the contract was signed called him and very matter of factly said 'When do you plan to deliver what was promised Chris?' It was a hard lesson still etched into corporate memory.

You can't think of business development or selling until you get the basics right. You have to build trust and that means putting the client first every time. It means making their life easier for them, not making it more difficult by failing to deliver the project.

You have to do the job really well first, then business development or selling becomes easy and a totally natural thing to do. It's too easy to sell once, but what sustains a business is winning again and again from the same client.

A Middle East client has been working with us for over five years, providing new projects worth over £10m because we really understand them and they totally trust the people working with them. It is our responsibility to be flexible and tailor how we deliver on each and every project – making life as easy as possible for them.'

Paul Tremble, Executive Director, WSP UK (a FTSE4 Good company).

Delivery as promised?

You delivered what you promised – well whoopee do!

Chris Daffy, author of *Once a Customer Always a Customer*

Delivery as promised = a satisfied customer

Satisfied clients are obviously better than nice customers who don't come back; but don't be fooled into believing that satisfied clients will be loyal clients.

After all, consider what 'satisfied' means. If you were satisfied with the service of the last restaurant or hotel you visited, I suggest you would describe it as OK, not bad, no better or worse than other establishments you've previously visited.

Organizations that aim to satisfy clients have as their objective to be described as 'OK'. They may very well hold on to a client that is satisfied for a while, but only until a competitor comes along and offers just a little bit more.

CASE STUDY Don't be a politician

'It really annoys me. Some suppliers are all over you with added value when they first win a contract, then they start taking you for granted and do just enough to avoid breaching the terms of the contract. They are all over you again of course when the next RFP is due. I liken it to politicians who are all over you when they want your vote.

Our best suppliers are delivering what they promised and then some. They keep finding ways to add extra value.

For instance when we had a major flood incident, the account manager of our communications supplier was on the phone to me immediately after he learned about it on the late night news. He told me he could have mobile masts in the area by first light the next day. OK, they got the extra revenues from the calls routed through the temporary masts but the emergency services had problem-free communications and they just took care of everything. It was one less thing for us to worry about.

Other great suppliers ask for our opinion on product design, invite us to meet their support people, keep us up to date with new innovations and stay interested in how things are changing for us. They show they care and are always interested in helping us.'

Simon Richardson, Procurement Manager, Devon and Somerset Fire Service

Principled Selling Tip: Delivery as promised is the minimum a customer expects. You have to deliver and then add more value for your key accounts.

The psychology of customer service

Daniel Kahnaman is an American psychologist and Nobel laureate famous for his work on judgement, behavioural economics and decision making. His work provides an insight into why Principled Selling customer service works.

Kahnaman's research demonstrated that there are two characteristics of people who affect decisions about buying or re-buying from a supplier. He refers to them as the 'experiencing self' and the 'remembering self'.

To distil his extensive research into a few words, it is what we *remember* about experiences that influences decision making, not the actual experience. Decisions to buy and to re-buy from a supplier are heavily based on experiences and memories. However, the full details of the experience itself fade quickly and it is the emotional memory of that experience which endures and affects our judgement.

The experience of a wonderful night in a restaurant is replaced by *'We came out, it was pouring rain, the car was 10 minutes walk away and the stupid restaurant didn't have any stupid umbrellas to give us, so we got soaked, and we'll never go there again.'*

See what happened? Despite it not being the responsibility of the restaurant to supply umbrellas, the embedded memory of that person is of the negative experience, and worse, that memory gets passed on to others! Consider this: suppose the restaurant had had a few cheap umbrellas and offered the customer one at cost for £3, refundable when the customer returns it. The whole experience now has been enhanced, locked into memory, and you just know the umbrella will be returned when they come back for another dining experience!

Kahnaman's research demonstrated that there are three experiences that are particularly remembered by customers:

- first impressions;
- significant events;
- last impressions.

First impressions

We have already established the importance of first impressions with regard to meetings and presentations. If your first impression fills a potential customer with confidence because you were better prepared, more professional, more interested and more engaging than your competitors, then that is what will be remembered rather than the finer details of a long proposal or pitch.

CASE STUDY

Open Field Agriculture Ltd is a supplier of seed and grain services that has an exceptional routine when they are visited by a customer. They have a small team who take care of all their visitors' travel arrangements. If someone is travelling by air or train, they liaise with their PA and make all the reservations, including hotels if required. They have a member of staff (not a taxi service) to make the transfer to and from the airport or station and their offices. A bottle of chilled water is provided for the journey. If the customer travels using their own car, a parking space right outside the main door is reserved, with a sign showing their registration number, name and company logo marking the parking bay. Directions from their point of departure right to the parking bay are sent well in advance. They do this so well that customers have even been known to take photographs of the sign.

On arrival at reception, visitors are welcomed by name and a newspaper is handed to them by the receptionist with words like, *'Your PA said this was your favourite newspaper and I believe you prefer tea with milk and no sugar?'* Not surprisingly this level of attention to detail makes a great first impression that is frequently praised by customers and remembered for a long time.

Significant events

Customers remember the added value you supply that is above and beyond what was contracted for. Significant events are potential 'WOW' moments where the customer gets a level of service that they didn't expect.

CASE STUDY

Dragon Fly Contracts Corp, which fit out and refurbish commercial offices, contact all their customer's onsite staff and those in neighbouring offices to explain about the work being undertaken. In the note they send they apologize for any inconvenience and provide a contact name and number to use during the time work is underway. It also explains that a free onsite car valet service is available in case anyone's car has been affected by dust from the work they carry out.

For long-term contracts they not only put their own site office at the location, they provide a fully furnished and equipped private office for the exclusive use of their customers whenever they visit. During site visits by clients, Dragon staff makes appointments to meet in that customers' private office.

Added-value events do take some thought and planning but rarely cost much compared to the overall project. They are events that customers remember and value long after the actual project is completed.

Last impressions

Fair or not, it is often the last transaction or experience that customers remember most, no matter how well you have performed what was contracted for.

CASE STUDY

'A great seminar, with lots I can put into practice when I get back to work. Event spoiled by tired-looking sandwiches and cold coffee at the end.'

Comment on training seminar feedback form

What spoils a relationship with a customer can be the smallest of interactions with an organization. A bad cup of coffee didn't really spoil a great learning experience but it is what the delegate will remember and tell others about.

Being kept on hold too long, calls not being returned, over-complex or incorrect invoices, and maybe even just a cold coffee are remembered as things that spoil an experience. There are hundreds of touch points between organizations and their customers where the experience can leave customers underwhelmed or thinking *'WOW, that supplier just keeps getting it right'.*

Principled selling tip: If your customer has had a bad experience, it is due to your neglect. If they have a good experience, it has been because of deliberate design on your part.

We actually don't choose between experiences. We choose between memories of experiences.

Daniel Kahnaman

In a world of indifferent customer service, the starting point for securing the business you get from your existing customers and clients is to deliver exceptional service right across your organization.

Everyone in the business needs to have a relentless passion to delight customers; it's the only way to secure long-term business.

Darren Laurie, Client Exec, Atos SA

Securing and developing key account relationships

Who are your key accounts?

All customers are important; they are all valuable to you. Even if the Pareto 80/20 rule holds for you – 80 per cent of your profit comes from just 20 per cent of your clients – there is still a lot of cash flow and potential with the 80 per cent who are probably not yet going to be your key accounts. Every client and every customer deserves to get great service from your company.

However, you simply will never have time to implement a detailed action plan to secure and develop relationships for every customer. Accounts nominated as 'key' are usually selected based on their:

- current revenue;
- potential revenue;
- referral value;
- strategic importance.

Your client base might be less than 10 customers or it might be hundreds, depending on your business. However many you select you need to be sure you have the time and resources to dedicate to producing and implementing action plans.

If you don't have a list of key accounts, start to compile one based on criteria appropriate to your business today. The effort and cost of winning new customers is considerably more than securing the revenue you already enjoy from your existing customers.

Principled Selling tip: It costs 6–7 times more to acquire a new customer than to retain an existing one according to recent research conducted by Flowtown.com.

If the most important strategy for your business right now is to maintain current revenue levels from existing relationships, then identify the customers most important to you in terms of the existing income they generate, and make them your key accounts.

If you are seeking to grow revenue from existing clients, identify those who you believe could buy more of the same products or services and those who you might cross-sell to; ie who could buy a wider range of products and services from you.

Key account management – action plan

There are five elements to an action plan for your key accounts:

1 understanding customer expectations;
2 mapping contacts and relationships;
3 objectively measuring the strength of relationships;
4 developing new relationships and opportunities;
5 taking action.

Customer expectations

You have to be sure you know what your key accounts expect regarding the products and services you provide to them. Just because a client happens to be in the same business as other customers doesn't mean they have the same expectations. Each key account contact will have their own 'icebergs', their own motivations, their own likes and dislikes.

Your first action in a key account action plan is to set out the expectations of all the key contacts. Be clear about:

● their expectations of your product or service;
● their expectations regarding how you communicate with them;
● their expectations of customer service.

The product or service you provide will have a different impact on people with different roles within your key account.

The senior executives are most likely to be interested in the strategic impact on the critical success factors affecting their business. The finance people will be focused on monitoring actual cost versus budget together with payment terms and processes. The head of a department you supply might be more interested in the impact on their team, on the unit's productivity and efficiency. The operators or users are most likely interested in the impact on them personally and their workload. The way you communicate with people has to match their preferred style. Some people like to have a meeting at the end of a project; some will want a weekly blow by blow account. Some people want face to face meetings, some are happy with an e-mail update or Skype calls. You just need to know who prefers what. Expectation of customer service may also differ between different people. Senior executives might be very happy if they never have to speak to your customer's support team, the front-line operational people may want to know someone is available 24/7 if anything goes wrong. Departmental heads might want a monthly meeting to discuss service issues. Again you need to be clear about every-one's expectations.

If a number of your colleagues interact with a key account, make sure you get their input regarding customers' expectations.

Relationship mapping

There are two tools we use to map relationships: a contact matrix and customer relationship matrix.

Contact matrix

The contact matrix is a template that allows you to identify all the influential contacts within your key account. It sets out who their point of contact is within your own organization and how the key individuals and influencers within the account like to be kept in touch.

FIGURE 10.1   Contact Matrix

Complete the following table identifying who you know and who you need to know (key influencers and individuals)

Client Contact	Title, role and responsibility	Primary internal contact	Frequency of contact	How? eg review meetings, lunch etc	Actions

There is a column for any actions required following on from the information you have captured. For instance you might find out you have a contact name but don't have any effective relationship at all. You might find there are relationships where you don't know the frequency of contact they prefer or how often they like to be updated. Your first action has to be to fill in any gaps in your knowledge.

It isn't unusual to find that there are too few people within your own organization who have relationships with individuals on the client's side. The better your people know more of 'their' people, the stronger the relationship will be and the more intelligence you can gather on 'under the iceberg' issues.

Customer relationship matrix

The customer relationship matrix is a tool that helps you to understand the perception of your company by individuals within your key account and any action that might be required to strengthen their perceptions.

FIGURE 10.2   Customer relationship matrix

STRONG

OUR REPUTATION

ALLY

YOU!

ADVOCATE

YES!

GRR!

DISSENTER

NO!

OPPOSER

WEAK   **THEIR ABILITY TO BUY**   STRONG

The vertical axis represents your reputation as a supplier with an individual, the horizontal axis reflects the level of influence that the individual has regarding decisions to buy or re-buy from you.

Take all the contacts you captured in the contact matrix and plot them on the relationship matrix according to which quadrant you think they fit.

The real power of this tool lies in the actions that it drives. You should have a strategy for each contact based on where you plotted them. Your strategy needs to take account of how the individual likes to be communicated with and how you can deliver useful added value through customer service and valuable content.

Advocate

An advocate is fighting your corner at a senior level when you are not present. Whenever an opportunity arises they think of you, they recommend you and they refer potential customers to you. Your reputation within their organization is closely linked to their personal credibility. Your strategy should be aimed at helping them to maintain their internal credibility and keeping them as an advocate.

Ally

An ally is positive towards you but has little or no influence over making decisions about buying or re-buying from you. Allies are sometime the individuals who are sent to represent senior executives at events you invite the senior people to. Sometimes too much time can be devoted to the ally relationship at the cost of relationships with senior executives, who are advocates. Your strategy should include maintaining your positive reputation and bear in mind that at sometime in the future they may be promoted to a position that gives them more decision making authority. You don't want an ally to become a dissenter.

Opposer

An opposer is someone in a decision making position or someone who has significant influence that actively works against any proposal to buy or re-buy from you. They might be motivated to oppose you by a bad memory of an experience or they may prefer another supplier for whom they act as an advocate. Your strategy should include working to at least neutralize their negative view about you and where possible encourage them to be an Advocate for you.

Dissenter

A dissenter often gets little acknowledgement or investment. They are usually operational people who use your products or services daily. What you supply affects their daily work routines. They might have little direct influence over a decision to buy from you but because they are negative towards you their constant complaints about you to senior management can eventually wear down your advocate's support for you or reinforce an opposer's view. Your strategy should include building relationship, understanding any issues and resolving any outstanding 'pain'. Work to turn them into an ally before they get promoted and become an opposer.

Customer relationship quotient

I've asked thousands of key account managers, partners in professional services firms and business owners about the strength of relationships between their organization and their key accounts. When I work with groups I go around the table and ask everyone to describe their relationship with their most important customers.

Their answers are always positive. Responses never take any thinking about and the replies flow as relationships are described as *good*, *great*, *fine*, *long-standing* or *loyal*. When I ask the next question, *'How do you know?'*, the room goes quiet.

What I'm seeking is some sort of objective measurement of how strong the relationship is but usually when I do get a response it is subjective: they have been customers for a long time; they always attend our events; they would tell me if anything was wrong; we do a great job for them. Finally I ask for a show of hands from anyone who was ever surprised to lose an important customer that they had done a great job for. Usually everyone's hand, including mine, goes up.

CASE STUDY

'They had been customers of my company for almost ten years, long before I even joined the business. The account was so important to my division that I had to make a presentation to the board every quarter on how things were going; it was worth around $2m a year. We had always had a great relationship. We were invited to their events, such as company hog roasts and even staff birthday and retirement parties. Our account manager was invited to the wedding of their buyer's daughter. Everyone got on really well and the contract had been renewed every two years without fail. I remember the day the 'Dear John' letter arrived only too well. It outlined that they would no longer be outsourcing their business operations processing and that the relationship would end when the contract was up for renewal in three months' time. It came from a C-suite executive none of us had ever heard of.'

Robert Lucado, Senior VP Sales, business process outsourcing company

I've heard many stories like the one above. It usually comes as a big shock to lose the customer and there is usually some sort of post-mortem to find out what happened. The investigations often find that in the early days there were a number of relationships at a senior and strategic level inside the account. Over the life of a contract, relationships become more operational and contact with senior people happens only when the contract is up for renewal.

What tends to happen is that operational people don't know about the strategic decision being made regarding changes to their business which might include fundamental reviews of business operations. By the time of a post-mortem it is too late for the supplier to have any influence or build new relationships. They often find that, even if the loss was inevitable, if they had been closer to the C-suite they would have at least received a warning well enough in advance to fill the hole the revenue loss would cause.

Measuring the strength of a relationship

FIGURE 10.3   Client relationship quotient

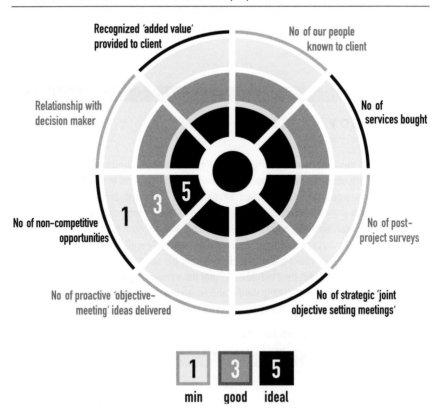

The client relationship quotient model helps you to identify actions that you can take to ensure no nasty surprises. The model brings objective measurement to how strong the relationship is with a key account and gives advance warning of any risks that could result in losing them.

The model works by scoring a number of criteria that would indicate how strong a relationship is. Actual criteria will change based on your own industry sector and the type of key account you are measuring. The principle is to have a set of criteria with three metrics that indicate a different strength of relationship and a score to indicate how you perform.

For example, for the criteria 'number of our people known to client' (one possible indicator of the strength of a relationship) the metrics might be 'less than 5', '5–10' or 'over 10'. The metrics equate to minimum, good and ideal relationships and each level is given a score.

The outer circle represents one point, the second circle represents three points and the inner circle represents the ideal score of five points.

The model shows actual criteria used by an engineering company. This is part of the template completed showing metrics and scores. The scores are transferred to the model to provide an instant graphical illustration of the strength of a relationship.

Below is an example of criteria you might use:

TABLE 10.1

Criteria	Score 1 point	Score 3 points	Score 5 points
Number of our people known to the client	Less than 5	Between 5 and 10	Over 10
Number of services bought	Between 1 and 3	Between 4 and 8	Over 8
Relationship with decision maker	Satisfactory	Good	Ideal
Number of offices we work with	1	2–4	5+
Have we delivered as promised?	Poor	Satisfactory	Excellent
Client perception	Weak	Satisfactory	Strong
Share of total client spend on products we could supply	< 25 per cent	25–50 per cent	> 51 per cent
Recognized as adding value	None	Some	Lots

With eight criteria the maximum 'ideal' score is 8 x 5 = 40.

Any score between 20 and 40 highlights potential room for improvement. Any score below 20 indicates the relationship might be at risk.

To arrive at the quotient, divide your actual score by the potential total score and multiply by 100. For example: 30/40 x 100 = 75 per cent.

(You will find more example criteria and strength of relationship templates when you download the Principled Selling Growth Model from **www. principledgroup.com/resources**)

When you have your own criteria you simply score the strength of the relationship using the metrics. When you have plotted the scores your results might look like this:

FIGURE 10.4 Client relationship quotient

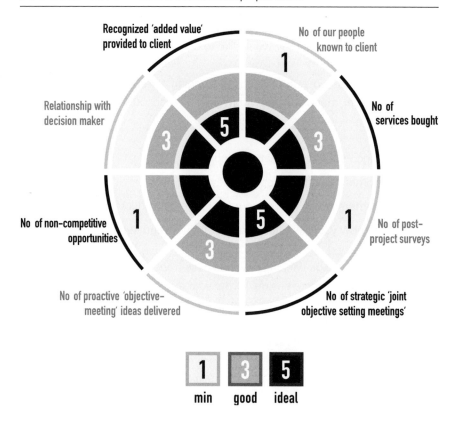

Identifying actions

Involve as many of your own people as possible in scoring the relationship and then identify any actions required. Your action might be to improve the score over a period of time or to take immediate action if any risks are highlighted.

With all three tools completed you should have a snapshot based on objective measurements of how strong the relationship is with your key account. More importantly, you have a list of actions designed to maintain or improve the strength of the relationships.

Developing opportunities

You have a great relationship with a great key account but you just know there must be more opportunities for you to sell to other departments, other offices or other companies in their group. Maybe you know that your key account is already buying services or products from your competitor!

Maybe you are missing out on opportunities that your key account would love to discuss with you. On every project where we conduct customer surveys on behalf of our clients there are always people who ask if we could get our client to contact them because they would like to discuss buying something!

Delivering great customer service and even doing a great job won't guarantee that you will win more business from your key account. Reasons for that include:

- You get pigeon-holed for what you supply.
- Your customer has other suppliers they like.
- Your customers doesn't know your full range of products and services.
- You don't know your own full range of products and services.

Just as you can manage winning new business from new customers, you can manage how you win more business from your existing key accounts. Winning more business from your key account in a Principled Selling way isn't about bombarding them with newsletters or just introducing a new product into a conversation at an account review meeting.

Winning more business in a Principled Selling way starts with a full understanding of your key accounts' 'horizon' issues. When you have that, you will be ready to motivate the right people to buy more from you.

Horizon issues

Horizon issues are about the future. They are the issues everyone knows are looming but for which there is no firm strategy in place to deal with them yet.

The better you understand your key accounts' worlds, the more you will begin to understand how you can help them.

Principled Selling Tip: Never start from a position of what you want to sell more of; start from understanding what would motivate your key customer to spend more with you.

There are two exercises that will help you to understand your key accounts' horizon issues. All you need to do is 'think like customers' and capture their critical success factors.

Critical success factors

Critical success factors (CSFs) are a limited number (usually between six and eight) of characteristics or conditions that have a direct and serious impact on the effectiveness, efficiency and viability of projects, programmes or even an entire organization. Any activities associated with CSFs have to be performed to the highest possible level of excellence in order to achieve the intended overall objectives.

There are four basic types of CSFs:

1 **industry CSFs** resulting from specific industry characteristics;

2 **strategy CSFs** resulting from the chosen competitive strategy of the business;

3 **environmental CSFs** resulting from economic or technological changes; and

4 **temporary CSFs** resulting from internal organizational needs and changes.

Imagine you are on the management board of your key account and ask: *'What are the critical success factors affecting our organization, this year, next year and in five years?'*

A tool to help you define CSFs is the acronym **PESTEL**. What will affect your key account under each of the headings?

Political

- bureaucracy
- corruption
- environmental law
- freedom of the press
- government type
- government stability
- labour law
- political change
- political stability
- regulation/deregulation
- social/employment legislation
- tariffs
- tax policy
- trade restrictions

Economic

- business cycle stage
- consumers' disposable income
- economic growth
- exchange rates
- GDP growth
- globalization
- GNP growth

- interest rates
- inflation rate (cost of capital)
- labour costs
- labour supply
- likely economic change
- unemployment rate

Social

- health consciousness
- population growth rate
- age distribution
- corporate responsibility
- career attitudes

- educational infrastructure
- social mobility
- employment patterns
- attitudes to work
- cultural taboos

Technological

- degree of automation
- emerging technologies
- impact of internet
- impact of social media

- rate of technological change
- R&D activity
- technology incentives
- technology transfer

Environmental

- weather
- climate

- climate change

Legal

- antitrust law
- consumer law
- discrimination law

- employment law
- health and safety laws

CASE STUDY

'We deliver parcels but our expertise is in logistics; we have many more ways we can help our customers than simple parcel delivery. We needed our key accounts to see us as a logistics partner rather than just a parcel deliverer. The answer was for our account mangers to really understand our customers' critical success factors. We got our account managers to give internal presentations about their key customers CSFs. This meant they got closer to senior executives within our key accounts and we developed our understanding to such a detailed level that opportunities we had missed just kept coming out of the woodwork. In the first year of applying a proper strategic approach to key account management we increased profit by over £2.5m. Our account managers also became valued strategic advisors to our key accounts.

Alistair Green, Sales Director, UK distribution and logistics company

When you know your key accounts' CSFs, how you can help them will become clear. Against the CSFs you capture, identify how you can help them to achieve their objectives.

Sometimes this might mean you need to adapt existing services and products or work on innovations which are driven by the long-term requirements of your customers.

Bringing it all together

Your key account action plan need be no more than two pages long. Remember that the action plan is not the client file; it is the place where you capture actions.

With all the information you have in mind start your action plan with a three-year vision for the relationship with your key account and a then 12-month target to implement specific actions.

Key Account vision – example

'We are perusing a comprehensive partnership with our key accounts based on an alliance for mutual success. Our aim is to make them more successful because they use our technology in all the regions in which they operate.'

Leading Bio-technology Corporation

Try to avoid using phrases like *to gain a greater share of the customers' wallet* or other financially related targets in your vision. Better financial performance is a by-product of delivering the vision when you focus on making your customer more successful by how you help them.

Your 12-month target is likely to be based on improving any gaps in your knowledge about the key account's world, improving the client relationship quotient, building relationships with new contacts and starting an M2M (motivate to meet) campaign with named contacts.

SMART action plans

Many readers will be familiar with the acronym SMART when it comes to objective setting. An objective is more likely to be achieved if it is:

- **S**pecific
- **M**easurable
- **A**chievable
- **R**esponsibility allocated
- **T**imebound.

FIGURE 10.5   Key account action plan

	Objectives	Actions	By when	Person Responsible	Date 1	Date 2
Loyalty Quotient						
Horizon Issues						

Name of Reviewer	Date of Review 1	Comment
Name of Reviewer	Date of Review 2	Comment

You can download a two-page blank action plan template from the Principled Group website.

Now motivate your key account to buy more

All you need to do is go back to Stage 1 of the Principled Selling Growth Model and identify the named prospects and specific contacts you will target in order to start building relationships with them using M2M marketing. Be clear about who you are targeting just as if your key account was a completely new customer. Many organizations have so many subsidiaries and business units that the reality is that, even if they carry the same name, they will effectively be a brand new opportunity for you.

Use all the valuable content tools, social media, networking and valuable content campaigns you have available to build trusted relationships prior to arranging an E^3 meeting where you will start the process of motivating your client to buy.

Summary

Somewhere today a competitor is planning to take your best customers away from you and make them their own dream clients. You and your organization need to be at least as committed to securing and developing relationships with your existing customers as your competitors are to winning their business. Never take existing customers for granted. Securing relationships from competitive incursion starts with delivering on your promises, all the time, every time and even then putting some WOW into the customer service you deliver. All customers and clients are important, but some become key accounts and you need to prepare an Action Plan to secure and develop your relationships with them.

You need to fully understand the expectations of your key accounts and map all the relationships of contacts who are or who could be influential in making decisions to buy or re-buy from you. Bring objective measurements to understanding the strength of existing relationships and understand the critical success factors of your key account over the next five-year period to help you identify how you might be able to help them achieve their objectives. Pull all the information into a two-page SMART action plan with your three-year vision for the accounts and 12-month targets.

Action points

- Who are your key accounts?

- Do something this week to impress them.

- Review your organization's commitment to key account management.

- Review how well you manage your customers' experience of doing business with you. Ask colleagues and customers for their honest feedback and who is doing better than you.

- Ask a client to visit your office and ask them to point out what you do well and not so well.

- Take action to correct any situation identified.

- If key account management and delivering a great customer experience are not priorities, start a discussion today about how to differentiate your company from your competitors.

- Ask if your company makes a great first impression, WOWs with significant events and always leaves clients with a positive memorable experience. If not – what will you do about it?

- Go out and meet your key accounts, start making objective measurements and make sure you know what your customers and clients expect from you.

- Map relationships and objectively measure how strong they are.

- Make sure you know your key accounts 'horizon' issues.

- Develop a SMART action plan for each key account.

- Download a key account action plan from **www.principledgroup.com/resources**

PART THREE
BUILDING A PRINCIPLED SELLING CULTURE

Principled Sellers thrive in a principled organization led by inspirational sales leaders. This part covers what you need to know to build a Principled Selling culture, how to tap into the hidden sales force in your organization and how to inspire others to win more business. It also explores the right Principled Selling attitude and how to make time to win more business without selling your soul.

CHAPTER 11

THE PRINCIPLED ORGANIZATION

Our chief want is someone who will inspire us to be what we know we could be.

Ralph Waldo Emerson

In the previous chapter we explored key account management, delivering excellent customer service, securing existing relationships and developing new ones. I mentioned that support from senior leaders in your organization is vital to getting key account management right. This chapter takes a look at how leaders can build a culture where Principled Sellers thrive and where the whole organization is actively involved in business development.

Topics covered in this chapter

- Principled Sellers thrive in principled organizations
- Leading a sales team
- Morivating 'unnatural' salespeople to sell
- Building a principled team

Principled sellers thrive in Principled organizations

Principled Sellers deliver more sales and more profit because buyers trust them to deliver on their promises. Buyers put a huge amount of faith and trust in Principled Sellers, even revealing their motivations, ambitions and fears, feeling sure that their supplier has their interests and success at heart. When you put that much faith in a supplier you really don't want to feel let down.

For Principled Selling to deliver sustained sales success, those members of the team out winning business need the support of colleagues and their leaders to also exhibit Principled Selling behaviours. That way you ensure that customers won't ever be let down by any part of the organization. Fortunately most organizations are driven by ethical principles and most people want to do a great job for their customers, so building a Principled Selling culture isn't too difficult.

Beyond good intentions

Many organizations have principles that guide the way they do business. Codes of conduct have become a legal requirement in some jurisdictions.

Sometimes, as evidenced by incidents like the Enron scandal and the more recent banking crisis, even organizations with established and fine sounding principles get their day-to-day behaviours wrong. I'm sure that when the principles were first written down there was every intention to abide by them; but somehow certain influential individuals forgot them or ignored them.

The financial institutions and organizations that failed, while they caused huge damage, are extreme examples of what can go wrong when there is a difference between the stated principles of an organization and the behaviours of some senior people in the business. If those people responsible for the demise had stuck to their principles, the problems that followed would never have occurred.

There are thousands of organizations that do live up to their principles, operating great businesses all over the world. They go beyond good intentions and bring their principles to life.

It starts with you

Whether you are freelance working on own account, part of a small business or part of a global enterprise, your personal behaviour is where to start. If you are in any sort of leadership position, your example sets the tone for your team.

CASE STUDY

'It's not just about the words; it's about my day-to-day behaviours. I have to demonstrate to our people every day that I live up to our principles and that I enforce them across the team. It's the only way we can have a culture truly focused on our customers. All the leaders in this business have to be the first to behave in the way we ask our staff to behave.'

Mike Bentley, Sales Director, JMCIT Ltd, *Sunday Times* Top 100 Company to work for

As you have come this far in a book about Principled Selling, I'm pretty confident that it is an approach that resonates with you personally. Hopefully the book has reinforced your commitment to taking a Principled approach and hopefully you have learned something that will help you to win even more business.

If you need some advice on how to build a Principled Selling culture in your team or in your wider organization, read on.

Leading a sales team

Whether you have a team of full-time sales professionals or lead a team of fee earners in a professional practice, the skills needed to build a culture of Principled Selling are those of a sales leader. Sales leadership is one of the hardest and most critical leadership roles in any organization. Leading fee earners and professional sales people has sometimes been likened to herding cats; they tend to have firm views and strong personalities.

It does require commitment to the more formal aspects of the business development process by applying the Principled Selling Growth Model; but knowing the right processes, skills and behaviours isn't enough. You also need to inspire others to apply them consistently and systematically.

CASE STUDY

'What did you do to my sales manager? He isn't taking over at customer meetings any more; he is so much more decisive and he spends more time coaching me than asking about my sales forecast. It's had a really positive impact on me and my results.'

Kerim Yilmaz, Senior Consultant, recruitment consultancy, Istanbul

What we did for the sales managers of that Turkish business was to help them become inspirational Principled Selling sales leaders. If you are responsible for the results of a team of sales people or fee earners, your job is to inspire them to implement Principled Selling and win more business. It makes winning business exciting, fun, builds high-performance sales teams and successful businesses.

First learn Principled Selling

The first step on the road to inspiring your team to win more business through Principled Selling is to be totally familiar with the concepts yourself and to enshrine them in your own working practices. Use the resources on the Principled Selling website, download the Growth Model and the various templates available and learn how to use them. You will need to provide guidance and personal coaching to help the team and individuals adopt the practices that will result in improved sales performance.

The tools you download become your sales management tools. Just like an individual uses them to monitor their own business development activity, you can use them to monitor your team's activity. Get everyone using the same approach and life will become so much easier.

Principled Selling Tip: Don't launch Principled Selling as another initiative; involve your team in developing an approach that best suits your organization.

If you don't have any existing processes for managing business development and sales activity, you can introduce the Principled Selling models and templates as tools to help you. Once you are familiar with them take care not to introduce them to the team in a Big Brother way. The main purpose of the models and templates is to drive the right activity and the right behaviours, so they should be seen as an aid to the team, not as another level of bureaucracy.

If your organization already has systems, then use the Principled Selling Approach to review what you already have. You can then discard elements of the old system which were not working well and keep the *best* of the old system. There may be some need to adapt the best into the Principled Selling approach, so this is a good opportunity to use the experience and knowledge of your top performers.

Inspiring the right behaviours

You don't have to have the title Sales Manager to have the responsibilities of a Principled Selling sales leader. Just as selling is a part-time role for some, sales leadership can also be a part-time role that comes along with other leadership responsibilities.

Focus on the right team behaviours

The best Principled Selling sales leaders coach their team in the behaviours that build trusted relationships with dream customers and clients. They frequently remind their team of the importance of long-term profitable relationships and how they result in sustained success for individuals and the organization. While a competitive spirit has its place, more important is the pride that the best Principled Selling sales leaders instil in individuals towards the team and the organization.

Every individual in your team has different motivations and aspirations. You can apply exactly the same questioning and listening skills you learned about in Chapter 7 to demonstrate genuine interest and understand the individuals on your team.

CASE STUDY

'I've never had any formal management training; I learned the hard way that people have to be treated as individuals. In a partnership it is particularly difficult because everyone you deal with as Managing Partner also owns a share in the business. If I want to influence behaviours in the firm I can't do that by dictate or by assuming the same message delivered in the same way will work for everyone. I work hard to understand every partner's motivations and even how they like to be communicated with. Leaders have to be genuinely interested in the individuals in the business.'

David Crabtree, ex-Managing Partner, Top 50 law firm

Adapting leadership and coaching styles

Because everyone on their team is different, inspirational Principled Selling sales leaders adapt their approach to coaching and mentoring accordingly. Just because your team are all sales people or all engineers or all accountants doesn't mean they can all be treated as one homogenous group motivated by the same things. Treat the individuals on your team as you would treat your best key accounts and apply the Principled Selling behaviours to your relationships with them.

Demonstrate enthusiasm and energy

The enthusiasm that a team or individuals have for Principled Selling and the energy they exert to apply it is directly correlated to the enthusiasm and energy displayed by their leaders. In high-performing teams no one wants to let the others down and no one wants to let the team leader down. The *buzz* of success is maintained in both good times and challenging times.

Encourage cross-team cooperation

When people operate in silos or there are any barriers between functional teams it has a negative effect on customers and your ability to win business. Inspirational Principled Selling sales leaders take responsibility for building internal and external networks, using online and offline tools to build relationships.

It is not inevitable that there is a clash between marketing and sales, or production and sales, or technical support and sales. It is part of the Principled Selling sales leader's job to set the best example of collaboration.

There are numerous teams and individuals that can help you and your team. The best way of eliciting that help is to reach out and see what value you and your team can add first and build trusted relationships.

Acting as a buffer

I was once told that bad news travels downwards. In other words my boss passes down to me the message passed down to her by her boss and I then pass the same message down to my team and so on. Some managers call it cascading information. Sadly my experience is that the message is sometimes filtered or given a personal slant that doesn't inspire those it is shared it with.

The best Principled Selling sales leaders act as a buffer between their team and the next level of leadership in the organization. They take the objectives and goals passed down to them, prioritize them to balance short-term and long-term objectives and turn them into inspiring and compelling visions for their team – an action equivalent to writing an e-mail from the future (Chapter 3).

They also represent their team to their next leadership level and demonstrate their pride in their team. They make sure that the voice of their team is heard and make sure any genuine concerns, as well as good news, are passed upwards.

Inspirational Principled Selling sales leaders don't see themselves as being stuck in the middle between two irreconcilable forces but as individuals who provide leadership in both directions.

Providing the right tools and systems

Nothing is quite so frustrating to Principled Sellers than to find that the processes and systems used by the organization *interfere with* rather than *support* their efforts. The Principled Selling sales leader has to provide the right tools and systems, encouraging the next level of leadership and other teams to provide support as well. The right systems support Principled Selling behaviours and manage out the wrong behaviours.

Recognition and reward

People repeat what is recognized and rewarded. If reward systems encourage the right Principled Selling behaviours, then those behaviours and the positive results they bring will follow.

You may not have the authority to implement reward changes at an organizational level but you can ensure any local recognition and reward encourages the behaviours needed to build long-term success for your team.

Be creative with any budget you might have for incentives, find ways to reward great customer service, recognize business development activity as well as actually winning business.

CASE STUDY

'We have lots of different ways of rewarding our staff, from individual rewards tailored to what motivates them to team rewards and company-wide incentives. It might be anything from a personal letter of thanks to a weekend break or more and it is all linked to customer service. Our sales people's reward package is linked to sales results and long-term customer feedback.'

Mike Bentley, Sales Director, JMCIT Ltd

Promote a 'we' not 'I' culture

Individual success is important, but not if it is achieved at the expense of sustained team success. When individuals are focused on external results like winning dream clients and giving great customer service so that customers buy and re-buy, individual performance morphs into team performance.

When I facilitated the board meeting of a well-known Rugby team, I met and worked with one of England's most successful rugby captains, Lawrence Dallaglio. I hope he learned something from me because I certainly learned lots from him. He inspires with almost every word and one thing he told me was that all he ever asked of a player is that they do what the number on their shirt asks of them and to do it exceptionally well. Anything else they can give to the team is a bonus. The team's objective is clear, to win. How they do that is by everyone playing their part exceptionally well so that team success is assured.

The best sporting leaders and the best inspirational Principled Selling sales leaders demand consistent high performance from individuals and create an environment where individuals can give their best for the team.

Richard Wylie, CEO, Principled Group Ltd

The responsibilities of the Principled Selling sales leader

Focus on targets

- Coaching the team and individuals to use the Principled Selling Growth Model to identify what level of business development activity is needed. Setting clear and realistic sales performance targets for numbers of named prospects, specific contacts, M2M activity, M2B meetings and key account management action plans to secure and develop existing key accounts.
- Sometimes setting targets that stretch the team and inspire achievement of the seemingly impossible.

Focus on measurement

- Selecting a few activities to focus on that are most appropriate to the teams' present strategy; ie focus on winning new business, securing existing business or creating new opportunities with existing clients.
- Inspiring individuals to see personal success in the context of team success.

Provide support

- Identifying the coaching and training requirements of individuals.
- Coaching the Principled Selling skills and behaviours to become 'the way we do things here'.
- Identifying opportunities for top performers, developing the skills of middle performers and managing poor performers away from a sales role.
- Proactively developing and encouraging internal and external networks to build cross-team cooperation based on how the team can help others to succeed.
- Delegating responsibility for leading presentation teams and key account teams to the best people for the job rather than doing it yourself.
- Avoiding taking over in client meetings and presentations.
- Debriefing and coaching post-E^3 meetings and presentations.
- Praising and encouraging Principled Selling behaviours.
- Instilling a feeling of pride in the team and organization.
- Dealing with any examples of bad sales practice swiftly and effectively to ensure no repeat.

Provide appropriate incentives and rewards

- Recognizing and rewarding Principled Selling behaviours as well as actual sales success.
- Rewarding best performers to encourage repeat behaviours.
- Setting expectations of success for middle performers.
- Linking rewards to customer service and customer feedback.
- Recognizing and rewarding commitment to key account management and willingness to develop opportunities for colleagues and the wider business.

Dealing with under-performance

The two types of people sales leaders say they have most issues with are the people who moan and are consistent under-performers; they are often one and the same person.

A huge amount of time and resources can be spent focusing on poor performers at the expense of time committed to middle and top performers. However there is often no strategy for dealing with either behaviour.

If you have invested in helping people to be Principled Sellers, providing coaching, mentoring, training and encouragement, then your strategy will have to be to manage them away from a sales role.

Principled Selling Tip: When considering moving poor performers into a different role or even outside the organization, always involve HR specialists so that you do things constructively and legally.

You and your organization simply can't afford to spend time with individuals not cut out for building trusted relationships and winning business.

Motivating 'unnatural' salespeople to sell

Many organizations have a hidden sales force made up of anyone with a client-facing or customer service role. There is potential to engage almost everyone in your organization in winning business and securing customers. Some professionals or technical people can be a bit more difficult to get onboard with the selling thing than others.

If clever people have one defining characteristic, it is that they do not want to be led.

Rob Goffee and Gareth Jones, Co Authors, *Harvard Business Review* article *Leading Clever People*

Clever people in the context of this book are those bright people who have a technical bias – the software geniuses, the designers, specialist lawyers, the innovators, technicians, research scientists and so on. There are all sorts of ways that people can be clever; some technical specialists need a different approach to how they are led than other smart people.

The good news about clever people in organizations is that they are already highly motivated. The last thing they need from leaders is motivation to get out of bed to do their job. The bad news for a leader is that they are motivated by the actual work they do and not always by what generates revenue and profit. I've yet to meet a lawyer, accountant, engineer or technician who qualified in their chosen profession in order to get involved in marketing or selling.

One of the most frequent questions I'm asked is *'Can everyone sell?'* After working with thousands of unnatural sales people over the last 15 years or so, I can report that there are some specialists who just don't like people. Just like I'd never advise anyone to have frontline customer service staff who don't like people, if you have clever people on your team who simply don't like people, make certain you never put them in leadership positions and furthermore keep them away from clients and customers.

Fortunately they are rare but if you do have them they are probably best suited to working on their own doing fantastic specialist stuff for your organization, its clients and customers. Your job as leader is to make sure they have the resources and freedom to do their job and that they work within the ethical rules and guidelines defined by the organization.

Today everyone, regardless of their job title, is in sales; they need to get some sales training. Bosses, put all your staff through sales training.

Paul McGee, Author of S.U.M.O. (Shut Up, Move On)

Most unnatural salespeople or technically-biased people fall into one of three categories:

1 those who are already Principled Sellers;
2 those who sell but are not Principled Sellers;
3 Those who think they can't sell or don't want to sell.

Full-time salespeople fall into the same categories.

Those who are Principled Sellers

Principled Sellers generate new business, secure existing relationships and develop new opportunities with existing clients based on implementing the

Principled Selling Growth Model. They build trusted relationships, share valuable content with their online and offline networks, earn the right to tell their story and motivate customers to buy using M2M valuable content campaigns plus M2B skills and behaviours. They attract dream clients and develop long-term profitable relationships.

Principled Sellers should be recognized and their good practice used to set the bar for how everyone should sell. When they win dream customers, as their leader you should shout the good news from the rooftops, ensuring everyone knows that this is how your organization does business. Use your best Principled Sellers to coach and mentor the not quite there yet people and make sure they know they are doing a great job. This will mutually benefit them and the organization.

Those who are not Principled Sellers

The worst type of non-principled seller is the one who meets or even beats their revenue targets. The downside is that they tend not to win dream customers and those that they do win can be high maintenance, unprofitable clients who have been sold the wrong products or services.

It isn't usually because they are not ethical people, it's normally just that they haven't been coached or trained in Principled Selling and haven't experienced how much easier and profitable the approach is. Leaders need to make sure that they are competent in the skills and behaviours they need and to strictly enforce the principles of the organization – even when this means reprimands and turning away an order or instruction.

Those who think they can't sell or don't want to sell

People in this category often hate the idea of being involved in anything to do with sales or business development. They hate it usually because they think they will fail. They believe the salesperson stereotypes and naturally don't see themselves in that role. They believe you have to be a certain type of personality or that if they 'sell' it will affect the trusted relationship they have with their clients or customers.

CASE STUDY

'I was asked to speak about Principled Selling at an accountancy conference in Lisbon. Before I went up onto the stage a conference delegate was telling me over coffee that her team could never be involved in selling and what was more she didn't want them to be. I crossed my fingers that she would at least have an open mind when it was my turn to speak. After my presentation she came up to me and said that she thought her people could be very good at what I had been talking about but would never do 'selling'.

'It brought home to me how powerful the stereotype of selling is. I spent an hour talking about winning more work by being a Principled Seller. This particular delegate didn't think of it as 'selling' at all.'

David Turner, Director, Questas Consulting Ltd., London

Building a culture based on principles

Principles are like a compass that points us in the right direction.

Dr Stephen Covey, *Principle-Centered Leadership*

Having the words isn't enough as Enron and the financial institutions demonstrated so clearly; but it is where it all starts. Your organization might already have stated visions, values and principles; if you haven't or if they might need to be reviewed here are a few things to think about.

I believe in honesty, integrity, trust and respect because these have served me well over the years. Without it you cannot sustain long-term success.

Sir Richard Branson, *Screw It Let's Do It!*

Principles are non-negotiable whatever the situation. Being a Principled Organization makes decision making for everyone easy. Just like a compass needle points to North and helps you to find your way out of a forest, principles point you in the right direction and help you make decisions about what actions to take.

Principles make a better business

CASE STUDY

Richard Branson's Virgin Group is one of the world's most trusted brands and has the same principles today that it has had since being founded in the early 1970s.

- Value for money
- Good quality
- Innovation
- Brilliant customer service
- Competitively challenging
- A sense of fun

Value for money – what we mean

- Keeping promises and being honest
- Transparent pricing
- No tricks or hidden charges
- Giving people more for their money
- Refreshing compared to others in the market

Good quality – what we mean

- Living up to people's expectations of us
- Earning trust, being honest and delivering on promises
- Excellent customer service
- Going the extra mile – small touches that mean so much
- Attention to detail
- Being self-critical

Innovation – what we mean

- Challenging conventions
- Not just big products and ideas but the little things that demonstrate personality
- Giving people what they want
- Innovative, modern and stylish design

Brilliant customer service – what we mean

- Friendly, human, relaxed, professional
- Listening to what customers say
- Respecting customers

- Staff being respected and valued and in turn passing that on to the customer
- Staff bringing their personality to work
- Staff being empowered

Competitively challenging – what we mean

- Answering a need in the market
- Inspiring customers by having the balls to fight rip-offs
- Fighting the establishment and showing that Virgin is a better way
- Promoting a 'them and us' spirit against the big boys
- Doing it with humour

A sense of fun – what we mean

- 30 years of music heritage
- Challenging convention and being daring
- Being irreverent = cheeky and tongue in cheek
- Making a point which people believe in
- Being human and having a sense of humour
- Being non-corporate and unconventional

I'm not suggesting Virgin's principles are right for you; only you and your colleagues can work out what your principles should be.

My daughter Claire works for John Lewis, a retail business that has sustained success based on principles first set out in 1929. They have a shared ownership scheme as lots of companies do and when I asked my daughter how they keep going from strength to strength she said, *'Pops, you know all those JL principles, that's what we all work to achieve every day and the results just follow.'*

As an inspirational Principled Selling sales leader you have to make sure you have set out the principles for your team and then do what Virgin do – the 'which means that' piece. Your principles shouldn't be open to interpretation, make it clear what you mean and what is non-negotiable.

What if I'm a lone voice?

Most organizations do have the best of intentions but for many reasons individuals can lose sight of what is right. Behaviours can creep in that you realize are less than helpful to you in your quest to build a principled team that wins more business through Principled Selling. It might be your peers or those several levels of leadership ahead of you that exhibit unhelpful behaviours.

In a very large organization you might have the freedom to run things how you want to, without interference so long as you bring in the required results. As long as you have influence over all the aspects of the operation that affect your ability to make Principled Selling work, it will be your team's results that speak loudest. Others across the organization will soon want to know how you manage to sustain good results and have customers that rave about you and your team.

It might be that the unhelpful behaviours of peers and senior leaders do interfere with your teams' ability to succeed. If that does occur, the best way to influence others is to apply the processes, skills and behaviours of Principled Selling to motivate them to actively support and commit to implementing the approach across the organization.

The trim tabber effect

Stephen Covey wrote an entire book, *The Eighth Habit*, on how people without authority can influence even major change inside organizations. In the book, he talks about the 'trim tabber' effect.

As you can imagine, large ships have huge rudders but to move those against the massive forces of water can take enormous effort and is very slow. However, on the tips of the rudders are much smaller flaps known as 'trim tabs'. The trim tabs are very easy to move, and when they do, they modify the flow of water around the rudder such that the water power moves the rudder and steers the ship.

In an organization, a trim tabber is someone who uses influence to facilitate change on a large scale.

Whatever position you hold, when it becomes obvious to peers and senior leaders that you have their and the organization's best interests at heart and that you provide value that helps them achieve their own goals and objectives, you earn the right to be listened to.

Building a Principled team

Customers come third

The key to success is how you treat your people.

Julian Richer, Richer Sounds, two times winner of UK's Best Retailer award

I once thought about writing a book with the title *It's all about people stupid*. It was around the time Bill Clinton said *It's about the economy stupid*. In my mind then was that the economic success of a business is inextricably linked to how an organization treats its people. I might not choose that title today but I'm as convinced as ever that you have to get the people thing right.

Every commercial organization has the same fundamental task – to exchange products and services for money. However complex, however shrouded in 'professional' mystique a business is, it all boils down to selling things that don't come back to customers who do.

For years organizations have broadcast that customers come first but then many don't deliver in a way that makes the customers feel that they are important at all.

To sustain success at exchanging products and services for money you have to put customers not first but third. You have to have to put people first, products and services second, then customers.

Putting the customer truly first means putting the employee who serves the customer 'more first'.

Tweeted by Tom Peters, author and management guru

When you get the people thing right, they will get the products and services right, they will look after your customers and your business with zeal.

Be a Principled Selling sales leader

Leadership isn't about position; it is about behaviours. A Principled organization is led by leaders who demonstrate that they are principled, who behave ethically and with integrity to do what is right in all situations. Leaders face many challenging situations and sometimes have to take tough decisions, but when all situations are dealt with based on ground rules that are non-negotiable, leading a business and sustaining success become a whole lot easier. Leaders ensure that there is an environment in which people can excel at making a contribution to business development.

You manage 'things' but you lead people.

Grace Hopper, US Naval Officer

Management is really important, it provides the disciplines needed to accomplish things. Without sound management no business could survive. Ticking the right boxes and having the right processes and systems is vital. Good management can keep things going but it is only leadership that gets people engaged and motivated.

Your management ability puts a companywide business development culture on everyone's agenda. Your leadership skills get everyone committed to it. As a leader you should use your management skills not in some sort of policing role but to make sure that systems and processes support your people to win dream customers and give great customer service.

A diet for inspirational Principled Selling sales leaders

Experience suggests that like most things, leadership can be simplified into behaviours that drive actions that make a difference. Building a business that lives by its principles and where everyone understands the impact they have on whether customers buy and re-buy just needs leaders who go on a DIET.

The DIET model shows each characteristic overlapping the other because the best Principled Selling sales leaders have to keep all four in balance in order to sustain improved performance.

Direction

Leadership comes from an ancient word that means to navigate at sea. I can't think of a better way to explain the number one priority of a leader – to show which way the ship is going. Sailors use navigational aids like charts and GPS, leaders use aids like vision, values and principles.

FIGURE 11.1   The management DIET

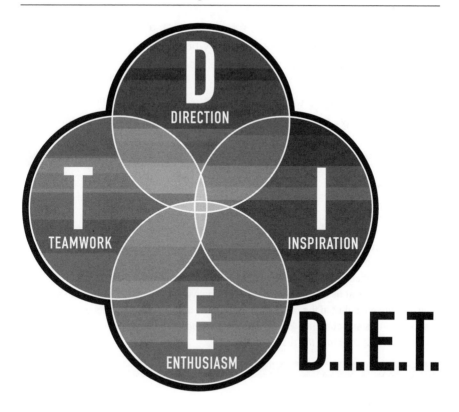

The best leaders have a clear idea of where they want to go and what the future looks like. They have their e-mail from the future that sets out what the ideal situation is three years ahead. They then share that with everyone in their team.

A vision paints a picture of the future in words so that it changes from being 'your' vision to 'our' vision. The key with sharing visions is to remember that no one ever gets out of bed to help you do deliver your dream unless it is their dream too. When you share your vision always make sure you answer the WIFM question – *what's in it for me?*

Inspiration

I'm not sure what it is but I could sure do with some.

Delegate commenting on inspiration at a recent leadership seminar

Inspiring others is about understanding the power of words. You don't need to be charismatic to inspire people, you don't need to be a great orator who can engage an audience of thousands. You just need to understand the power of words and then choose your words wisely when you communicate. To get the best from people you need emotional intelligence.

Words have the power to inspire or deflate, to calm or inflame, to create positive or negative responses that have a direct impact on performance.

CASE STUDY

During their preparation for the 2012 Olympics, champion swimmer Rebecca Adlington and heptathletes Jessica Ennis and Louise Hazel had to deal with derogatory comments being made about their appearance. *'Most things written about me are not swimming-related'* said Rebecca Adlington. Adlington, Ennis and Hazel knew their athletic performance was at risk if they took notice of negative comments but went on to say that they took huge comfort in the overwhelming number of positive comments they had from their supporters and coaches. *'It's the positive comments that will help our performance, so we learn how to ignore the rest'*.

Whoever wrote *'sticks and stones will break my bones but words will never hurt me'* really didn't know what they were talking about. Words have a physiological effect on people. So much so that they can drive outstanding performance or kill performance dead in the water. Words can affect a person's performance for an hour, a day or even a whole lifetime.

Dr Joseph Le Doux discovered that the human brain filters all inputs through the amygdala (the emotional brain) before the rational brain kicks in. Depending on the words used, the amygdala releases hormones, a chemical cocktail that affects how we respond. It's partly why the human species has survived; we have a finely tuned emotional response to threats, most commonly known as the *flight or fight* response. It's what kicks in when people who hate the thought of public speaking are put on the spot by a manager to give a presentation.

Their heart rate speeds up, their mouth goes dry, and sometimes blush patches appear around the neck. All physiological responses caused by the release of adrenalin and cortisol into the bloodstream.

There's a lot more science to it than that, but I like to think of the effect of words in terms of 'ouch' or 'wow' moments. Sometimes words sting and sometimes words inspire.

CASE STUDY

J D Wetherspoon plc is a British pub chain. Founded as a single pub in 1979 by Tim Martin, the company now owns over 800 outlets. The J D Wetherspoon name comes from one of Martin's teachers in New Zealand who said that Martin would never make anything of himself. The words meant so much to Tim Martin he named his business after the teacher who spoke them.

Dear Big Boss, remember when you weren't the big boss and how good it felt when the big boss said your name. Do that.

Tweeted by Vala Afshar, Chief Customer Officer, Enterasys Networks

If you are in any sort of leadership position you really need to understand the effect of words and your team's performance.

Everyone enjoys being recognized, especially from someone they look up to and respect. Don't be stingy with your praise. Catch someone doing something right today. You'll be surprised at the difference in makes in their life – and yours.

Ken Blanchard, *The One Minute Manager*

Enthusiasm

What about one leadership style – Enthusiast in Chief?

Tweeted by Tom Peters, author and management guru

Enthusiasm is inspiration plus excitement and it is contagious. Teams and individuals with a spark of enthusiasm can overcome the most serious of obstacles and deliver outstanding performance.

Cheerfulness in adversity is a core Royal Marines principle.

Warrant Officer Steve Hill, Instructor, Commando Training Centre, Lympstone

FIGURE 11.2   Demonstrating enthusiasm

| Preparing to do battle | The thrill of victory | The agony of defeat |

The cartoon above was given to me by the managing partner of a leading law firm. He said that it portrayed the typical partner he reported to when he started out in law. He gave copies of it out to his staff, telling them to shoot him if he ever looked like he was turning into that sort of boss!

Some people in leadership positions underestimate the effect they have on people just by the mood they portray. Some bosses are drains and some are radiators. Drains, take away everyone's energy just by being in the room. For them every silver cloud has a black lining; they see the negative in everything and make sure they share negativity around. Often we try to avoid drains because when you spend time with them it can really spoil your day.

Radiators on the other hand fill people with energy and a 'can do' attitude. People want to be around them because just by being in their presence they feel better and more enthusiastic themselves. If you are not sure that it matters much, ask your customers whether they like to deal with people for whom everything seems too much or with people who seem to have boundless energy and give them great service.

Enthusiasm doesn't have to be about being animated and waving your arms around. Quiet, considered and serious people can and do show their enthusiasm by the tone of their voice and subtle body language signals like smiling from time to time.

Teamwork

The most effective and efficient way for a Principled Selling sales leader to get things done is through teamwork.

The benefits of teamwork include:

- synergy whereby the results obtained by the team working together are greater than if the individuals worked alone;
- the empowerment of individuals to innovate and deliver great customer service;
- the cutting across of silos, which in turn encourages multidisciplinary work;
- the fostering of flexibility and responsiveness to change;
- the promotion of a sense of achievement, equity and camaraderie that keeps people motivated.

High-performance teams outperform groups of people doing their own jobs in isolation every time. Whether it's two people or 2,000 people, being part of a team is invigorating and performance enhancing.

Members of high-performance teams:

- support the objectives of the team – with enthusiasm;
- respect colleagues;
- listen to each other's ideas and opinions;
- support colleagues;
- share information freely;
- praise each other;
- can be depended on;
- are proud to be members;
- accept responsibility;
- accept constructive criticism;
- use campaigning politics to influence;
- achieve individual high performance;

Summary

Principled Sellers thrive when they work for a Principled Organization. Leaders have to ensure that the organization practises what it preaches. Fine words about values or principles mustn't be there as a veneer or for cosmetic reasons to hide the real truth about what it is like to do business with a supplier. Building an ethical organization, one where people don't have to sell their soul, requires deliberate action on the part of leaders and it starts with the leaders themselves. Leaders make sure that processes and systems support the people out winning business and everyone serving the customer, and provide the leadership that builds high-performance teams. They also engage the hidden sales force so that everyone in the organization plays their part in winning more business and securing existing customer relationships.

Action points

- Ask your team if the organization has processes and systems that help them to do the best for customers and clients. If they say *no*, start to remedy any shortfalls within the next month.
- Ask your team if you demonstrate the behaviours demanded by the organization's values and principles. Ask for specific examples of good behaviour and poor behaviour. Don't get defensive, but act to amend any shortcomings in your behaviour, starting now.
- Put Principled Leadership on your agenda and provide support, training and coaching for all managers.
- Do something to inspire your people every day.
- Seek out someone on the team you haven't met with for a while and ask them if anything organizational is blocking their ability to succeed. If there are any obstacles, fix them.
- Praise someone today for something specific they did well.
- Say *thank you* to people on your team who do their normal job day in, day out.
- Change any words you use that might drain the energy from people into words that will radiate enthusiasm.
- If you don't yet have a high-performance team, use the information in this book to design new ways of working so that you provide the support, coaching and training to ensure people excel at Principled Selling.
- Visit **www.principledgroup.com/resources** for more resources that will help you to develop your ability to be an inspirational Principled Selling sales leader.

CHAPTER 12

ATTITUDE AND MAKING TIME FOR PRINCIPLED SELLING

I would be doing you a disservice if I didn't mention how much the way you think impacts on your success as a Principled Seller. You have probably heard before that *attitude is everything* and it is my experience that it is true. Having a positive attitude about winning business is easy when things are going well, but how do you stay positive about the future in more difficult times?

Topics covered in this chapter

- Thoughts become actions; actions become behaviours
- Coping strategies – shut up, move on!
- Making time for Principled Selling

Thoughts become actions; actions become behaviours

Attitude is a little thing that makes all the difference.

Winston Churchill, British statesman

It might seem brutal to point it out, but there are too many well-qualified experts in their field who don't have enough business to allow them to practise what they love to do. There are too many salespeople falling below target and too many great companies underperforming. The one thing they have in common is that they all need more customers to exchange money for their products or services.

Principled Selling will definitely help you to win more business – but only if you implement it. If you want to know who is responsible for implementing it, take a look in the mirror. I know Principled Selling works, I know it's helped thousands of business people, professionals and professional sales people to win more business, but here's the deal: you have to be committed to it.

Many people I meet have spent years honing their technical or professional skills. Often they are members of professional associations that demand CPD (continuous professional development) in order to make sure their skills and knowledge are right up to date. Business owners with a passion for what they do, whether they happen to be printers or electronics engineers spend years gaining experience and hours staying on top of their subject. This book and the resources on the Principled Selling website will help you but it's not enough, you need to develop your own and your teams' CPD of selling.

Some readers may still have to come to terms with the need to sell or help others to do so.

Do I *really* have to learn how to sell?

Selling is a noble, honourable normal business activity that got itself a bad name. Even if selling is never going to be your full-time role or your favourite way of spending your time, the best way to be successful and enjoy it is to be personally committed to learning how to sell and commit your organization to providing the environment where Principled Sellers thrive.

Selling becomes easy when you deliver what you promise and do a fantastic job for your customers. When you make the life of a customer easy why wouldn't they come back for more?

CASE STUDY

'Without long-term commitment to making Principled Selling work, any existing sales process and culture will always drive behaviours right back to the status quo.' Before Principled Selling, the sales training I have experienced in my career, however well-founded, failed to achieve complete or sustainable results because there was no real commitment and no ongoing support. They were one-off interventions.

'The best organizations adopt moral principles with their staff; the natural behaviours this generates are then applied to customer relationships, which in turn lead naturally to winning and retaining the best clients. Individuals and their organizations need to constantly improve how they win business and how they service clients. I've proved that by personally by winning multiple contracts' running into hundreds of millions of pounds, year after year, in the private and government sectors.'

Darren Laurie, Account Executive, Atos SA

Pygmalion

If you think you can you will be right; if you think you can't you will be right.

Henry Ford

Everyone can be better at selling and enjoy it more if they decide that they can.

Pygmalion in the Classroom, based on the research by Robert Rosenthal and Lenore Jacobson, came to the conclusion that student achievement mirrors teacher expectations more than it does actual student ability. When others believe images of how things should be, they become self-fulfilling prophecies – the tendency of people to perform in accordance with what is expected of them as well as their own expectations of success or failure.

Believable, positive expectations result in positive results. Unbelievable or negative expectations create the opposite. This phenomenon is called the Pygmalion effect.

It's about how you think

There really isn't any mystique about what is happening with self-fulfilling prophecies. It boils down to the fact that what we think and say is followed by actions and behaviours which become habits that determine outcomes.

CASE STUDY

'I came to the launch of the latest management initiative to increase sales through networking with low expectations and didn't expect anything to change. I'm pleased to report that I was inspired by what I heard about social media and I'm going to sign up for Twitter today.'

Feedback from delegate at Principled Selling event

If you go into something deciding it won't work for you, then everything becomes a negative. No matter what evidence is provided, no matter how much support is offered if you decide something is not going to work, you will be right. To make success with Principled Selling a self-fulfilling prophesy, you might start by thinking: *'I'm not 100 per cent sure how to make it happen yet but this looks like it could help us win more business.'* You then take some of the actions suggested at the end of each chapter. You download the Principled Selling Growth Model and the various templates available and introduce some colleagues to them. Discussions begin about the Principled Selling approach, live information goes into the model, valuable content is found, social media networking starts and before you know it you are meeting senior decision makers in named prospects that could become dream clients. You *think* Principled Selling can help you win more business, action and behaviours follow and you *do* win more business.

CASE STUDY

'I'd arranged an appointment with one of my best clients because they wanted to speak about the fees I'd proposed for legal advice on a franchise termination. They wanted me to sharpen my pencil and look again at the amount. I'd already decided what I was prepared to reduce my fees to but fortunately had a coffee with one of my colleagues beforehand. She asked me why I'd quoted the level of fees I had, so I told her. When I finished she said 'well you've convinced me, why don't you go and say that to the client; I did, got the instruction and I didn't give any discount.'

Partner, UK law firm

In Chapter 11 we looked at how the words you use can affect the performance of your team. Words can also affect your own performance. Your ability to win more business is affected by the words others use and, more importantly, the words you say to yourself.

Top athletes train their minds just as much as they train their bodies because they know that what is going on in their head can make the difference between a gold medal and no medal. Sport coaches talk about *the inner game*, others talk about *the inner voice* or *self-talk*. Your inner voice has a lot to do with whether you will be good at and enjoy that part of your business life that involves selling.

The bumble bee's weight-to-lift ratio is all wrong and there is no way it can fly according to scientist Antoine Magnan; but no one ever told the bumble bee.

Jack Russell, *Don't Tell the Bumble Bee*

CASE STUDY

'After seven years as a tax techie I was petrified of even picking up the phone to speak to clients, I never thought I'd ever be any good at selling. I would describe myself as shy and introvert. Carl (franchising partner) must have seen something in me because he asked me to go to a few franchising events and I found I enjoyed meeting people. I got thrown in at the deep end one day and ended up speaking at one of the events. Carl is so good at networking and selling and I was worried I'd let the firm down. Anyway I got through it and found that attendees started to come to ask me for advice. I've won clients since on my own and suddenly I realized that selling isn't about pretending to be someone else, it's just about helping people and communicating. Now I love being involved in anything to do with business development.'

Emma Manning, Tax Manager. Dennis and Turnbull, Charted Accountants

It's not confidence; it's competence

Some of the most successful salespeople I have met are professionals and individuals with a technical background. Their assuredness about their technical ability provides them with the confidence to deal with all sorts of challenges, including learning how to sell. Once they know what to do they really fly because they start from the premise of doing a great job for their customers.

For years professionals and others with a technical bias have been told that they are not the sort of people who would be good at selling (or at leading people for that matter). I guess that if bumble bees could understand, and if someone told them often enough that they couldn't fly, they wouldn't even try.

Anyone who has been told often enough that they aren't supposed to be good at selling or that they don't have the 'right' personality profile will start to tell themselves that it must be true. As the words we hear are our own words, that *inner voice*, we tend to believe them.

The human brain is fascinating and complex, but it doesn't have the capacity to differentiate between what is real and what is merely a perception. People are very good at rehearsing negative outcomes in their head for instance; imagining situations that haven't happened and not likely to happen. The problem is that when we rehearse negative outcomes our brain responds as if what we are rehearsing has already happened. It is a brain function that was helpful when we were being chased by sabre-toothed tigers but is a less useful when we are about to give a presentation convinced it is all going to go wrong.

CASE STUDY

'At our annual conference the Senior Vice President of sales told the delegates that she needed the support teams to be more involved in selling to our key clients. I immediately panicked. I felt my heartbeat increase as I "knew" I would fail at sales.

Then I refocused on what she was saying about the extra support and training that we would get. There was an input from a technical colleague I admire, who said he'd panicked at first but had taken to it like a duck to water. I found myself thinking if he can do it so can I. Panic over.'

Team Leader, Digital Systems, semiconductor manufacturer

Another fascinating thing about the human brain is that you can change the way it responds to a thought in an instant. Followers of NLP (neuro-linguistic programming) will know the technique as 'reframing' and it is hugely powerful.

Reframing is easy. You just change the words in your head and your body responds accordingly. 'I can't' becomes *I can*. 'It won't work' becomes *Let's give it a try*; 'I'm nervous' becomes *I'm excited*.

'I can't sell' becomes *I can be good at Principled Selling.*

Whether you are an athlete or a business person who needs to win business, what you rehearse in your head will affect your performance.

CASE STUDY

'I'm just finishing my law degree and have been fortunate enough to land a job with a Top 5 "magic circle" law firm. It's been made clear to me from the start that I'm expected to be a brilliant lawyer and, if I want to get on in the firm, I also have to be good at business development – winning and keeping clients. I'm really looking forward to that part of being a lawyer. Doing a great job with great clients in a great firm, who could want more?

Haidee Barratt, Law Graduate of Christ Church College Oxford

I just know Haidee is going to have a brilliantly successful career!

Business people, technical people and professionals already have the ability and skills they need. It's just a matter of adapting and improving existing skills, not adopting completely new ones. Then it's a matter of practising those skills and keeping them razor sharp and ready to put to use when they are needed.

Coping strategies – shut up, move on!

We all have bad days. Being positive about winning business on a good day is easy, but it's on the bad days that we need coping strategies. I love what Paul McGee, the SUMO guy, has to say about dealing with the challenges life throws at us.

Shut Up, Move On (SUMO) is saying a number of things. It is meant as an encouragement that whatever your past experiences, your future doesn't have to be the same. *Move On* is asking you to look at your future so that you see the possibilities that lie ahead rather than being stuck in the reality of your current circumstances. It's a call to action to do something, to *move on*.

Hippo time

A hippopotamus is known for wallowing, so I call human wallowing 'hippo time'.

Before people can SUMO they may need time to wallow, to be left alone to dwell on things for a while. As human beings we are by nature emotional. A life without experiencing emotional highs and lows would be boring and bland. In order to move on you need at times to acknowledge the emotions you are feeling. To make the most out of Hippo time and prevent yourself wallowing for too long here are seven questions to ask yourself that will help you to SUMO.

1   Where is this issue on a scale of 1–10? (where 10 = death)

2   How important will this be in six months' time?

3   Is my response appropriate and effective?

4   How can I influence or improve the situation?

5   What can I learn from this?

6   What will I do differently next time?

7   What can I find that it positive in this situation?

Reproduced with kind permission from Paul McGee, Author of *S.U.M.O.*

People are always blaming their circumstances for what they are. I don't believe in circumstances. The people who get on in this world are the people who get up and look for the circumstances they want, and if they can't find them, make them.

George Bernard Shaw

Getting started

The time to start Principled Selling is now.

When you decided to read this book you probably did so for one of two reasons: you need to win more business personally or you lead a team that needs to win more business. Like most people you and your team are probably under time pressure and you might wonder how to fit in everything that needs to be done in a world of multiple priorities.

We all have the same 24hrs available to us, it's what you do in those 24hrs that makes the difference.

Richard Denny, Author of *Selling to Win*

Anyone who lives in a world where everything is a priority has no real priorities. All the best business people, professionals, salespeople and sales leaders set goals for themselves and their team, plan, set priorities and manage the time available accordingly. No professional services firm would survive without the ability to project manage client work for instance, so the skills to prioritize do usually exist. It's just that sometimes peoples' day-to-day priorities are not linked to their business goals and objectives.

Making time for Principled Selling

Rocks

When Stephen Covey, author of *The Seven Habits of Highly Effective People*, filled a pitcher full of rocks in front of an audience, he asked if it was full. When the audience responded with *Yes*, he poured in some pebbles. He again asked the audience, *'Is the pitcher full?'* After the audience replied *Yes,* he poured in some sand and asked again if it was full. The audience said *Yes* and he then, finally, poured in water. When he really couldn't get anything more into the pitcher he asked the audience what point they thought he was making.

'You can always do more, you can pack more into your day', were typical of the responses.

'No' said Stephen Covey, *'the point is you have to get the rocks in first'.*

When you are planning how to use your time the rocks are the priorities that will propel you towards achieving your stated goals and objectives. You have to get the rocks into your diary before you do anything else. Rocks are immovable objects because they represent the priorities that will most quickly help you to achieve your goals and objectives.

There is an old proverb, 'the road to hell is paved with good intentions' and the real risk is not lack of time but that you or your team will find something else that you or they would rather do than be involved in winning more business. It can also feel a bit more comfortable to stick with what you know rather than try something new, even though in your heart you know it isn't going to achieve the results you need.

Ultimately it takes less time to do things right than it does to do things wrong.

W. Edwards Deming, father of Kaizan 'continuous improvement'

Your Principled Selling rocks are business development activities – diarizing meetings to select named prospects and named contacts, diarizing time to develop valuable content and to network, and doing those things that will motivate potential dream clients to meet you. Put rocks in your diary to start key account action plans and for building relationships with new named contacts.

Make your training and development 'rocks' too. No matter how long you have been involved in selling or leading others, you should take every opportunity to further hone your skills. Practice makes perfect is an old adage. Actually the truth is that practice makes permanent and it is really easy to be very busy doing the wrong things.

Generals' shouldn't prepare to fight the last war.

Anon

There is always a risk that if we have been successful in the past, we will think that what worked then must work today and all we need to do is more of the same. It is often the reason senior executives and sales leaders dismiss social media out of hand. The most successful Principled Sellers and sales leaders put continuous learning on their list of important things to do and put rocks in their diaries to achieve it. They then harness new ideas such as social media and find ways to use it.

Summary

Success in sales needs all the right processes, skills and behaviours; in addition it needs the right attitude. Like all professional skills, Principled Selling needs commitment to keeping up to date and honing your abilities. Take care with what you think and what you say. The Pygmalion effect is powerful and can determine your ability to succeed based on the expectations you have of yourself and your team. When you implement Principled Selling and see it work for you, your competence and therefore confidence will grow. Be aware of your 'inner voice' and have coping SUMO strategies for those difficult days. Lau Tzu wrote *'the journey of a thousand miles starts with one step'* – take the first step towards winning more business without selling your soul today.

Action points

- Be honest with yourself and ask people you trust whether your attitude to selling, or life in general is 'can do' or 'can't do'. If you tend towards a 'can't do' attitude, then write down the words your inner voice tells you and reframe them into more helpful words.

- If you need some serious reframing then engage a coach to help you.

- At the next team meeting share five things you have learned from this book with your colleagues and coach a team member on the Growth Model. The best way to learn is to teach others.

- Read a book from the suggested reading list on the Principled Selling website. Take three things you learn from the book and make an action plan to implement them.

- Identify the important 'rocks' that you need to diarize, put them in your diary and start your Principled Selling journey.

- Check the resources section at **www.principledgroup.com/resources** and sign up for the regular newsletter that will keep you right up to date with the latest Principled Selling and Sales Leadership thinking.

FURTHER READING

Blanchard, K and Johnson, S (2011) *The One Minute Manager: Increase productivity, profits and your own prosperity*, HarperCollins, London

Bounds, A (2010) *The Jelly Effect: How to make your communication stick*, Capstone, Chichester, UK

Branson, R (2006) *Screw It, Let's Do It: Lessons in life*, Virgin Books, London

Covey, S R (2004) *The 8th Habit: From effectiveness to greatness*, Simon & Schuster, London

Covey, S R (2004) *The 7 Habits of Highly Effective People*, Simon & Schuster, London

Daffy, C (2001) *Once a Customer, Always a Customer: How to deliver customer service that creates customers for life*, Oak Tree Press, Cork, Ireland

Deming, W E (2012) *The Essential Deming: Leadership principles from the father of total quality management*, ed J Orsini and D Deming Cahill, McGraw-Hill, New York

Drucker, P (2007) *The Essential Drucker*, Butterworth-Heinemann, Oxford

Goffee, R and Jones, G (2009) *Clever: Leading your smartest, most creative people*, Harvard Business School Press, Boston

Green, C and Howe, A P (2012) *The Trusted Advisor Fieldbook: A comprehensive toolkit for leading with trust*, Wiley, Hoboken, NJ, USA

Howell, M T (2010) *Critical Success Factors Simplified: Implementing the powerful drivers of dramatic business improvement*, Productivity Press, New York

Jefferson, S and Tanton, S (2013) *Variable Content Marketing: How to make quality content the key to your business success*, Kogan Page, London

Kahneman, D and Tversky, A (eds) (2000) *Choices, Values and Frames*, Cambridge University Press, New York

Lewes, B A (2012) *The Magic of NLP Demystified*, 2nd edn, Crown House, Carmarthen, Wales

Mattern, J (2003) *Grace Hopper: Computer Pioneer*, Rigby

McGee, P (2011) S.U.M.O.: *Shut Up, Move On: The straight-talking guide to succeeding in life*, Capstone, Chichester, UK

Peters, T (2010) *The Little Big Thing: How to pursue excellence at work*, HarperBusiness, New York

Richer, J (2009) *The Richer Way*, 5th edn, Richer Publishing, London

Rosenthal, R and Jacobson, L (2003) *Pygmalion in the Classroom: Teacher expectation and pupils intellectual development*, Crown House, Norwalk, CT, USA

Russell, J (2006) *Don't Tell the Bumble Bee*, Jack Russell Books, Topsham, Devon, UK

Scott, D M (2011) The New Rules of Marketing and PR: How to use social media, online video, mobile applications, blogs, news releases, & viral marketing to reach buyers directly, 3rd edn, Wiley, Hoboken, NJ, USA

Sun-Tzu (2006) *The Art of War*, Filiquarian Publishing, Minneapolis

Townsend, H (2011) *FT Guide to Business Networking: How to use the power on online and offline networking for business success*, Financial Times/ Prentice Hall, Harlow, Essex, UK

If you would like to implement Principled Selling, the team at Principled Group would be delighted to help you.

Principled Group Ltd
Haunton Grange
Haunton
Tamworth
Staffordshire
B79 9HN

www.principledgroup.com

or contact David Tovey directly at: **david@principledselling.co.uk**

Group companies
Principled Selling Ltd
Questas Consulting Ltd
Valuable Content Marketing Ltd

INDEX

NB entries in *italics* indicate a figure or table in the text

kshal